The Cross of Christ

ANDREW MURRAY

Marshall Pickering

Pickering & Inglis Ltd
Marshall Pickering
34–42 Cleveland Street, London, W1P 5FB, U.K.

Copyright © 1989 Marshall Morgan & Scott Ltd
First published in book form in 1989
by Pickering & Inglis Ltd
Part of the Marshall Pickering Holdings Group

Clarion Classics are published by the Zondervan Publishing
House 1415 Lake Drive, S.E., Grand Rapids, Michigan 49506
North American Edition Copyright 1989 by the Zondervan
Corporation Grand Rapids, Michigan

British Library CIP Data

Murray, Andrew, *1828–1917*
  The cross of Christ
  1. Jesus Christ
  I. Title II. Series
  232

  ISBN 0–551–01860–7 (Marshalls)
      0–310–56122–1 (Zondervan)

Text set in 10/11pt Times Roman by Watermark, Hampermill
Cottage, Watford. Printed by Richard Clay Ltd, Bungay,
Suffolk.

CONTENTS

The Baptism of Fire

Introduction

*The Cross
the Power of God*

*'The word of the cross ... to us who are being
saved it is the power of God.... We preach
Christ crucified ... the power of God.'*
1 Corinthians 1:18,23,24

Power belongeth unto God. We can have only so much
power as God gives us. And he gives it to us only as he
himself dwells in us, and is waited on to work. In the
great work the church has to do in this world, as in our
personal spiritual life, all experience and increase of
power depends entirely upon our standing in the right
relation to God, upon our knowing the way in which his
power works, and the conditions under which it is given.
In our text the Holy Spirit points us to the cross, with its
shame, and weakness, and death, and tells us the word
of the cross, the crucified Christ, is the power of God.

God's thoughts are not as our thoughts: there is no higher or harder lesson to learn than that the cross, as it reveals man's sin and curse, and God's love and redemption, as it calls us to the fellowship of Christ's suffering, and the conformity to his death, as it crucifies the flesh, and separates from the world, is the only path to the power of God.

Power: there is nothing men seek more earnestly. In the pursuits of war or peace, in politics and commerce, in science and art, everywhere power is sought. The same is true in the church. How many addresses are given in answer to the question: Why has the church so little power over the masses? Why cannot it cast out the demon of modern society? Why can it not conquer the world? And when the feeble spiritual life of believers is pointed to as the cause of the lack of power in the church, this only raises new questions. Why, with so much preaching and prayer, so much earnest pursuit after holiness and strength, why do believers not rejoice more in the strength provided by God?

To these questions many answers are given. One is, the lack of faith. If we only understood better in the surrender of perfect impotence to trust God and wait on him, he would work in us and through us. Another answer is, the lack of the fullness of the Spirit. If the fire of heaven burnt within us, and we were men full of the Holy Spirit, the world would soon see and be compelled to confess the power of God. Still another is the absence of the unity of the body, of the humility and love to which alone God's presence is promised.

All these answers have their truth, and yet each one suggests a new question: But why is it that, with so much desire to do so, we cannot exercise the mountain-moving faith? Why, with so much prayer for it, do we not receive and prove the fullness of the Spirit? Why, in the presence of the united forces of the world and Satan, why, that we do not lay aside our divisions, and in the power of the love that dwells in us, seek our strength in unity? Yes, why, that with all our seeking of strength, it is still so little found.

May it not be that we have not gone deep enough, to the very root of the evil? The cross is the power of God! We have sought to believe in and expect the power of God. But have we understood that Christ crucified cannot be the power of God to a believer except just as far as he is crucified with him, actually living a life of full crucifixion to the flesh and the world? We have longed for the fullness of the Spirit. But did we remember that it was through the cross Christ won the Spirit? 'He was crucified through weakness, yet he liveth by the power of God.' The weakness of the cross fitted him for receiving the power of God. We have prayed for the manifested unity of believers and the gift of an overflowing love. But did we know that it implied such an utter death to self and its life as only the death of the cross can give? The cross, the crucified Christ, is the power of God. We have asked God to give us the blessed fruits of the tree of life, faith and love, and the Holy Spirit – but we refused to tarry under its shadow, and to wait for them there where alone God will give them. 'The word of the cross is the power of God.'

Believers: who mourns the lack of power, who prays and waits for power, who pleads God's promises and secretly wonders that the answer is so small – God is calling us to the secret place of power. We must begin to study Christ on the cross more intensely. We must find out what the dispositions were that gave the cross its value, and what the elements of divine power that lay under its weakness. We must choose to the very utmost to be like him, bearing the cross, crucified to the world. In the likeness and weakness and death which we shall taste in the fellowship of the crucified, a secret door will be opened into the place of God's power which all our willing and running never could discover.

Christ crucified, the power of God! We always consider that the expenditure of power ought to be in exact proportion to the greatness of the work to be done, or the value of the results to be obtained. And what was it that justified God in choosing this way for the display of his power – his own Son dying on the cross? It was indeed a work of which God knew that nothing less would suffice, and that its outcome would more than outweigh the sacrifice he made. And what was the work? Listen.

God had made man in his own image. God's creating love had brought forth a creature of such wonderful perfection that it could be the vehicle through which the life of God could manifest itself, and the very likeness of God could be seen on earth. Man was destined to be God's delight, to live in his fellowship, to bear and show forth his glory, to be the habitation and manifestation of all his perfection.

Sin entered and death came because of sin. Man died to God and the holy, heavenly life he had been destined to. He fell under the power of the flesh and the world, and his soul, instead of living in blessed dependence upon God, established a kingdom of its own, where everything was subservient to its own rule and interest. Man, and with him the world he was to have ruled and blessed, fell under the power of Satan, who now became the god of this world, and maintained his reign of darkness and sin in defiance of God.

The destiny to which God had created man in his image was so high and divine, the love in which God had longed indeed to lift him into a participation of his own blessedness and glory was so infinite, that God counted no price too great for the restoration of his lost creature. God so loved the world, that he gave his only begotten Son. The power of sin that had to be conquered was so terrible that nothing but his death on the cross could accomplish the deliverance. In the bearing of its curse the righteous demand of the law was satisfied, and the punishment of sin fully borne. The sacrifice had its value from the humility and obedience and willing surrender with which the Son as man yielded himself to God's will. And so the cross is the power of God in both respects – in the atonement it made, and in the spirit in which it was borne, in that which gave the suffering and death its worth.

The preaching of the cross the power of God! As the cross reveals the atonement and redemption of Christ, God's free love and everlasting life as its gift, it breaks the heart, and draws the sinner to repentance and faith. It is the entrance into the new life. As the cross is known and believed, the heart is drawn to the crucified Christ himself, to find in him and the way in which he walked, the path and the power to a life well-pleasing to God. As the terrible power of the flesh, and the world, and self are felt, and our perfect impotence is discovered, it is seen that nothing less than the cross, the crucified Christ, can give power to overcome. We see Christ by his atonement so put away sin, that we are freed both from its condemnation and its dominion. In the faith of this deliverance we are led to see deeper into the awful nature of that self that has exalted itself against God, and found its expression in the whole spirit of the world. We see, too, the absolute need of a divine humility, sacrificing itself like Christ on the cross, to become willing that God again may have his place and his honour. And as in ourselves this power of God in the weakness of the cross is revealed, we reach the place where the power of God can do its mighty work in us and through us.

The cross the power of God. Nothing less can do the work. So terrible is the reign of satan, of sin, of self in the world that only the divine power, not of the omnipotence, but of the love of God in its humility and suffering, can reach or conquer the heart. Let us begin to believe that as it is triumphed on calvary, it can triumph in us and around us. Let us see and acknowledge the cause of all weakness and failure – the spirit of the cross, the spirit of a crucified life, was lacking. And let us, as never before, gaze on the crucified One with loving, longing hearts, till he takes us into the full fellowship of his death.

Christ crucified, the power of God! That is more even than the cross the power of God. It points to the living one, who has taken us up into the fellowship of his death, and longs to reveal it fully in every one who is willing for it. It points to him who liveth in us, and waits for us to say how far we are ready to follow him. Shall we not confess how little we have known the power of his cross, as the utter death of self. Shall we not say how little we understand what it means, and beseech him to make us worthy to enter into perfect fellowship with him. Shall we not at once surrender ourselves in impotence to his mighty working, and begin to believe as never before in the cross as the mighty power of God working in us.

To all who are seeking for the power of God, the power of the Holy Spirit, in their lives or their work, I bring the solemn question: Have we remembered that it is from the glorified Christ the Spirit comes, and that the glorified Christ is the crucified Christ, whose whole life and disposition was a giving himself to the cross? As the Christ of this spirit and disposition is preached as the way to God, as this spirit of the cross is manifested in the church and its preachers, as Christ crucified, rejected by the world, and meekly giving himself to the death, is loved and followed, is shown forth and seen in his witnesses, the power of the cross and the power of the Spirit will again be known in their wondrous unity as the mighty power of God.

Chapter 1

The Spirit Leads to the Cross

'Christ, who through the eternal Spirit offered himself without blemish to God.'
Hebrews 9:14

Every spirit creates its own body, as the appropriate and necessary manifestation of its hidden nature. Every plant is the body or shape in which the spirit of life that was hidden in the seed reveals itself. Every fruit is the embodiment of the spirit or nature of the tree on which it grows. It is the same with man, the features of the face become the expression of the hidden spirit that dwells within. All our conduct has its hidden root in character, in the disposition and desire of the inner man. Life always clothes itself in a shape corresponding to its real being.

The cross of Christ is the highest expression of the

spirit of Christ. The cross is his chief characteristic, that which distinguishes him from all in heaven and earth, that which gives him his glory as mediator on the throne through eternity. Until we truly know the spirit that led Christ to the cross, we neither know it nor him. There are many aspects from which the cross needs to be studied, but it is only as we enter deeply into its spirit that its full glory will be defined. We may look at it as the wisdom of God, the wondrous plan he devised for our redemption. We may regard it as the power of God, and seek to know it by its mighty working and the blessed work it has accomplished. We may look at it in the light of man's sin, of the curses of the law, of its perfect atonement, of the love of God and Christ that shone forth in it, or of all the life and joy it brings the sinner, from each new point of view new glory will shine forth. And yet the chief thing which is its most essential element, that which gave it its value in God's sight, and for which he chose it, that which made Christ crucified the wisdom and the power of God is the spirit of the cross, the spirit that during his whole life animated Christ and led him to it. This is what we need to know.

When we have discovered what the spirit was that led Christ to the cross we shall see how this is only one part of the great subject, the Spirit of the cross. We shall see how the Holy Spirit of Pentecost is still the Spirit of the cross. As he led Christ up to the cross, he flows forth from the cross to us as its purchase and the impartation of its power. And we shall then further find that as he led Christ to the cross, and the cross led to the giving of the Spirit, so the Spirit will always lead back to the cross again, because he alone can reveal its meaning or communicate its fellowship. The Spirit leading Christ to the cross: the cross leading Christ and us to the outpouring of the Spirit: the Spirit leading us back to the cross! These are the three parts of our subject.

What is the spirit that animated Christ in giving himself up to the cross? Scripture gives many answers. Obedience to the will of the Father is one. Love to men is another. The purpose to conquer and destroy sin is another. And yet each of these suggest the deeper question: Why was it the will of the Father that he should die? Was there anything in the necessity of things that led to this being the only way by which man could be saved? To this Scripture gives the answer: It was only by death that sin could be atoned for, and its power broken. And once again the question rises: But why and how? The judicial aspect of the death as atonement is one side; the vital aspect of the death as a victory and deliverance is its complement. Scripture does not teach that with the bearing of the cross and the atonement the meaning of the cross is exhausted; that when we trust to its finished work our only relation to it is that of grateful confidence with what we are to it. No, it tells us that in the most intimate spiritual fellowship the cross is to be our life. We are to live as crucified with Christ: we are to walk as those who have crucified the flesh and can conquer it in no way but by every hour regarding it as crucified. We are day by day to bear the cross, and to glory in it, because each moment our relation to the world is to be that of men who are crucified to the world, and know and feel the world crucified to us. If the spirit of the cross is then to make and mark the only true christian life, if this is to be our likemindedness to Jesus, we want to know what it was that made that spirit of the cross the only power by which Christ could win life for us, or by which we can possess and enjoy life in him.

The true answer will be found if we consider what the need in man was which the cross was to meet. There is no passing from one state of life to another but by dying to the first. By sin man died to the life he had received from God, and by dying to it he lost it. If he was to be delivered out of his sinful life, and to be restored to his first divine life, there was no passage out of the one to the other but by dying to it. The voluntary surrender of everything belonging to the old life as having the stamp of sin and the curse upon it, the choosing of death to all that had been counted life, was the only way back to the

life of God. This would be the only atonement man
could ever make for his sin.

But that atonement man could not make. He wanted
both the will and the power. His sinful nature could not
choose this death. And even if he had given his life up to
the death, there was within him no new life that could
rise up out of the death. And yet the law remained and
still remains unalterably true: no passing out of the life in
sin to the life in God but by dying to it.

What Adam could not do, what no man can do, Jesus
Christ has done. He has opened the passage out of this
life in the flesh to the life of God and heaven by dying to
it. He came and identified himself with us in all the con-
sequences of our sinful state so closely that he lived and
died as if he had been a sinful man. He took exactly the
place that a sinner ought to have taken. He did and suffered all that we ought to have done and suffered if we
could have won back our way to God. In the power of
the eternal Spirit by which he offered himself a sacrifice
unto God, and by which he was raised again, his death
was the victory over death and an entrance for his human
nature too into the life and glory of God. And because as
Son of God we belonged to him, and God had appointed
him our second Adam, and in his assuming our human
nature he had made himself one with us, his passage
through death to life could avail for us, and his spirit
could enable us to walk in the way he had opened up.
Through a new spiritual death (unto sin) and a new
spiritual life (unto God) we can come back and reach
again the divine life we had lost in Adam.

The path in which Jesus Christ walked had its value in
the first place, not from the amount of suffering, or the
actual surrender to death, but from the disposition
which animated him. And that disposition was not something strange or different which came in his last hour, but
what animated and inspired him through the whole
course of his earthly life. And it is only as this spirit
becomes the animating principle of the life of the
believer that the thought of being 'crucified with Christ'

can have anything like true meaning. It is only as the same spirit which led Christ to the cross is the spirit of our life, that the power of the cross to separate from the world and to sanctify unto God can really be known.

This disposition or spirit, of which the cross is the expression, this readiness to give up all that is of human nature to the very death to have it lifted up into the life of God, we have looked at from its human side. If we ask the question, Whence had our Lord this mind which was in him, and the power at any cost to carry it out, we have the answer in our text: 'who through the eternal Spirit offered himself without blemish unto God.' It was part of Christ's humiliation as man, and one of the chief elements of his perfect likeness to us, that he became dependent upon the Holy Spirit for all his light and strength to know and do God's will. It was in the power of the Holy Spirit that he offered himself unto God. The cross, with its protest against the world, its honour to the righteous judgment of God, its endurance for the salvation of men was simply the embodiment, in visible shape, of what God had to endure at the hands of men, of how he hated the sin, and yet sacrificed all to save the sinner.

It was this eternal Spirit that was in Christ from his birth that taught him to say – words that contain the seed of the obedience of the cross – 'I must be about my Father's business.' It was this Spirit that led him in baptism to humble himself to be treated a sinner. It was this Spirit with which he was then afresh baptised, to fit him for the death to which the baptism had set him apart. It was this spirit that led him into the wilderness, there to resist and overcome and begin the struggle that ended on calvary. It was through this Spirit that he was led on step by step to speak of and meet and bear all he had to suffer. As it had been in the prophets, 'the Spirit of Christ ... when it testified beforehand the sufferings of Christ', so it was through the eternal Spirit that all was fulfilled and accomplished. The Spirit of God, dwelling in flesh, leads inevitably and triumphantly to the cross.

'What God has joined let no man put asunder.' The cross is the power of God, and the Spirit is the power of God. The cross is the most perfect expression of the mind of the Spirit, of what he asks and how he works. God taking possession of human nature to free it from sin and fill it with himself, can do so in no other way but by slaying it. There is in the wide universe no possibility of liberation from the power of sin, but through personal separation from it in entire death to it. What God demands the Spirit works. He worked in the man Christ Jesus, the spotlessly holy one, who yet, in virtue of his union with us, and our forerunner in the path to life, needed to die to sin. He works it now as the Spirit of Christ in each of his members.

Let all who desire to be filled with the Spirit stay and worship here. The Spirit leads to the death on the cross. As he had nothing higher to do for us in Christ ere he quickened him in the grave, he has no higher work he can do for the believer than to lead him into the perfect fellowship of the cross. Pause and worship here, and pray to know what it means. Have you yielded truly to the Spirit, to lead you as he led Christ along the path to the cross? Are you seeking for the fullness of the Spirit in full unity of heart with his one purpose, to be in you the crucifixion Spirit as he was in Christ? To you, as to Christ, this is the sure, the only path to glory.

Chapter 2

The Cross Leads to the Spirit

*'Jesus of Nazareth ... being delivered by the
determinate counsel and foreknowledge of
God, ye have taken, and by wicked hands
have crucified and slain: Whom God hath
raised up ... Therefore being by the right hand
of God exalted, and having received of the
Father the promise of the Holy Ghost, he hath
shed forth this, which ye now see and hear ...
Therefore let all the house of Israel know
assuredly, that God hath made that same
Jesus, whom ye have crucified, both Lord
and Christ.' Acts 2:22–36*

One of the chief lessons we need to learn in regard to the
cross of Christ is its close and inseparable connection
with the Spirit of Christ. The right apprehension of this

truth is of vital importance, both in the life of the believer and the work of the church. We may imagine that our trust in the cross and its ever-blessed atonement is clear and full, or we may strive earnestly for its holy imitation and partnership, and yet, unless we yield to the Holy Spirit to teach and strengthen us, and communicate the 'hidden wisdom of God in a mystery' to us, our faith and our practice may stand very largely in the power of men. Or, on the other hand, we may be striving in every possible way for the power of the Spirit in life and work, and wondering why our prayers are so little heard, and the reason may be simply that, with the church around us, we have not understood how the cross, with its testimony against the world that rejected Christ, with its revelation of God's curse on sin, and its confession of the power of sin over all that is nature, with its crucifixion of all that is of self and the flesh and the world – how this is what the Spirit seeks to work, and what we must yield ourselves to, if he is to reign in us. The life of the cross and the life of the Spirit must always grow in equal proportion; they are vitally and inseparably one.

In our last meditation it was: the Spirit leads the cross. Now we turn to the converse: the cross leads to the Spirit. Come and see how true this is of Christ, of the believer, of the sinner, of the preacher.

1. The cross leads to the Spirit. See it in our blessed Lord himself. The cross, with its victory over sin, was Christ's path to the Spirit. See how this is the one thought that comes out in Peter's address: it is Jesus, the crucified one, who has been exalted and has received from the Father the Spirit. It is from the crucified one in glory that the Spirit comes. The cross was to him the path and the power through which alone he could receive the Spirit to pour out.

And how then? We can look at it in different aspects. We can speak of the cross as the ransom, the price he paid for our redemption, and his receiving the Spirit from the Father to give us, as what he had purchased and earned. When the curse had been borne, the barrier that prevented God's dwelling in man was removed, and our Mediator could claim the Spirit for us. Or we can regard the cross as the death in which he himself and his obedience were perfected, and he as man was fitted to receive the fullness of the divine Spirit and glory to communicate to us. He became obedient unto death, the death of the cross, therefore God hath highly exalted him. Or we can think of the cross and its death as the only path which he, as our head and forerunner, could open up for us to die out of the old life of nature, and enter into the new life to God. The completeness of his entrance into our death, even unto the very uttermost, was his perfect entrance into a fullness of the Spirit that could over-flow unto all his people.

These different aspects have each their unspeakable value. The first, the legal one, points us to that substitution and atonement which is the foundation of the sinner's peace and hope. The second, the personal one, shows us what it was in Christ that gave his suffering such value, and made him our leader and example. The third speaks of the vital connection, in virtue of which the cross shows the very path, the only disposition, through which we can become fully fitted for the Spirit's indwelling.

We need to combine all these, looking now at one and then at another, if we are fully to realise the deep and most needful truth: The cross, the cross alone, the cross borne, and experienced, in its power to slay, is the only path to the throne or the Spirit of God.

2. The cross leads to the Spirit. Look at it in the disciples. It was their fellowship with Christ in the crucifixion that fitted them for the baptism of the Spirit. What was it that separated these hundred and twenty men and women from all the world, and made them the worthy recipients of the pentecostal gift? They had followed Christ, even to the cross; when all had rejected him their heart clung to him. When he had died and their hopes appeared extinguished, they still clung to him, the

crucified one. The meaning of the cross they did not yet understand, but he who died upon it was their only life or hope – as far as love could do it they were one with him in his shame and rejection, and he made them one with him in his death and its infinite blessing. All their training for the baptism of the Spirit had led to the cross and been completed there. The cross leads to the fullness of the Spirit.

Let all believers who long and pray to be filled with the Spirit take this to heart. We must be lovers of the cross. We must first trust it, and then share and bear it. What the cross did for Christ, as it gave him through death release from the life of humiliation that now he might 'live unto God', the cross must do for us too. As we yield to the Holy Spirit, as far as we know him, and live the life he gives, of men who have been 'crucified with Christ'; 'who have crucified the flesh'; 'who are crucified to the world', the Spirit in his fullness will come and possess us. The death to self and its will, to the flesh, to the world, which the cross gives is the only path to the Spirit. The more complete the deliverance we get from the old life at the cross, the more entire the death to all that is nature, the more whole-hearted the desire for conformity to Christ's death, the surer and the richer the fullness of the Spirit.

3. The cross leads to the Spirit. This is the path too for the unconverted sinner. It is the cross that works both that conviction of sin and that faith in God's mercy that receives the promise of the Spirit. Read our text over again. See how Peter's preaching all gathers round the two thoughts – how God honoured Christ and how man rejected him. Jesus, whom they had crucified and slain, God had raised from the dead and placed on the throne, and given the Holy Spirit to pour out. In the crucified one they saw their sin and guilt, they saw God's mercy and power to save. It was the cross, with its revelation of man's sin and God's love, that brought them to share with the disciples in the outpouring of the Spirit.

The last words of Peter's address give us the very

essence of gospel preaching. 'Know that God hath made that same Jesus, whom ye have crucified, both Lord and Christ.' In the history of the Congo Mission there is a touching narrative of a missionary wondering and mourning over the lack of blessing after five years' preaching. After much thought and prayer he was led to adopt the tone of that verse – to charge the heathen boldly with their rejection of God's Son. The word came with power. When Stanley passed again, some time later, he saw and testified to the extraordinary change. It is the preaching of the cross in this double aspect, as the revelation of man's wickedness, of the very spirit of the world and all who are in it, in rejecting Christ, however ignorantly, as well as of the mercy of God offering pardon and the Holy Spirit, that God will bless.

4. The cross leads to the Spirit. This is the great lesson the preacher needs to learn. See this in the preaching of the church at Pentecost. Through the man who glories in the cross the Spirit will work. Listen to Peter, not only on the day of Pentecost, but in Solomon's Porch (Acts 3:14–26), or before the Council (4:10; 5:30), or in the house of Cornelius (10:39); it is ever the crucified Lord he preaches, and God owns. And so at all times of revival, when the Spirit of God is poured out, it is in connection with the preaching of the cross in its twofold aspect – as revealing man's sin and God's mercy.

But that is not all the preacher has to learn. Let him mark well – the blessing of the preaching does not depend only on the matter, but the man. If Peter had not been baptised with the Spirit of the crucified one, he could not have preached him aright in the power of the Spirit. And if Peter had not followed Christ to the cross, and had not, in the midst of failure, held fast to him, even through shame and death, he had not received that Spirit of power. It was what the crucified Lord had done for him in leading him to the cross, that fitted him for what he did from the throne. To be a witness for a crucified Christ needs two things: it needs the very spirit and disposition of the crucified Lord on earth, and then

the Spirit of the glorified Lord from heaven. The cross is
the dark and dead-looking bud, the Spirit the bright and
fragrant flower. The cross is the sour, unripe fruit, the
Spirit the ripe grape yielding its living sap, the wine of
the kingdom. As in Christ, so with the believer and the
penitent sinner, but above all, in the preacher it must
ever be, the cross leads to the Spirit.

The Holy Spirit is as much the gift of the Father to his
church as the Son. 'When the fulness of the time was
come, God sent forth his Son ... that we might receive
the adoption of sons. And because ye are sons, God hath
sent forth the Spirit of his Son into your hearts.' What
can it be that both in the personal experience of godly
believers, in the life of the church at large, in the work of
the church in the world, the joy and power of the Holy
Spirit is so little known? May it not be, is it not possible,
that the true cross, not only the cross that is trusted in,
but the cross that is borne and experienced in crucifixion
power, the cross that is witnessed to by a spirit and life
that the world can see, is not known and accepted? It was
the real cross, with its suffering and shame, that led
Christ to the throne and the fullness of the Spirit. In no
other path can we reach what he reached. The cross
means for him, and for us, a cross to be borne, a death,
in which he and we are crucified together. Let all who
pray for revival and the outpouring of the Spirit pray for
a revival of the religion of the cross, with all it meant to
our Lord; the revival of the Spirit's mighty working will
follow soon. It is God's unalterable law in delivering us
from sin and the world: the cross leads to the Spirit.

Chapter 3

The Spirit
Reveals the Cross

> '*We preach Christ crucified ... the wisdom of God ... we speak the wisdom of God in a mystery, even the hidden wisdom ... which none of the princes of this world knew: for had they known it, they would not have crucified the Lord of glory.... But God hath revealed them unto us by his Spirit.... Now we have received, not the spirit of the world, but the spirit which is of God; that we might know.*' 1 Corinthians 1:23–24; 2:7–12

The Spirit leads to the cross. The cross leads to the Spirit. And then the Spirit leads back to the cross to reveal its full meaning, to communicate all the power of its death and life. As each seed bears fruit after its kind and of its very own nature, and the fruit in its turn again becomes a seed, so the Spirit of Christ was the hidden seed-life of which the cross was the fruit. And the cross again became the seed of which the Spirit is the fruit. And, once again, the Spirit in the believer, and the church as a whole, is the seed, of which the conformity to the cross and the death of Christ is the fruit. It is the great work of the Spirit to fill the world with this blessed seed, everywhere to reproduce the image and the likeness of the crucified Lord. The highest work of the Spirit is to reveal the cross – the wisdom and the power of God.

How strongly Paul puts this in the second chapter of 1 Corinthians. After he announces that his preaching had not been in the wisdom of men, or in excellency of speech, or in persuasive words, he teaches how vain it would have been to do so. 'We speak the wisdom of God in a mystery, even hidden wisdom.' If excellency of speech or persuasive words of men could have converted or enlightened men, who could have done this better than he who spake as never man spake. But the princes of the world understood him not. God hides his mystery from the wise and prudent, and reveals it unto babes. The natural man receiveth not the things of the Spirit of God: spiritual things can only be spiritually discerned. The same Spirit who, apart from and contrary to all human wisdom, led Christ to the cross, must even so, apart from and contrary to all human wisdom, still lead men to the cross. The power to apprehend and accept and rejoice in the cross, the Spirit alone can give. The divine wisdom that devised, and in due time revealed, the cross, can alone reveal it in the heart. What a change would come, and what a blessing it would be, if the church really believed this truth. Let us look at what its effect would be.

1. The cross is the wisdom of God in a mystery: the Spirit of God alone can reveal it. How this would humble and then help the believer in glorifying in the cross. It would humble him as he felt his own utter helplessness to receive what the cross offers, or to yield what it claims. There are many Christians who heartily confess that

there is in them neither righteousness nor strength. They admit that their natural powers of heart and will are impotent to do what God demands. But they do not know that, as entirely as they lack righteousness and strength, they lack wisdom too. Just as unable as they are to render a spiritual obedience to God's will, are they to have a spiritual apprehension of it. Did they believe this, they would recognise how a mystery of divine wisdom needs a divine illumination to receive it.

Have we not often sought by earnest thought to enter more deeply into the significance of the cross? Have we not, as we got a glimpse of some aspect of its glory, gone from book to book to find out what it really means? Have not some given up hope that words like 'I am crucified with Christ'; 'the world is crucified to me'; 'baptised into his death'; 'dead unto sin and alive unto God in Christ' should ever become truly intelligible and helpful? Is not the reason for all this that we want to grasp the hidden wisdom of God with our little mind, and forget that the Holy Spirit wants to give it into the heart, and into the inner life, in a way and in a power that passeth knowledge?

Let anyone who desires, possibly as he reads this book, to be brought into fellowship with his crucified Lord, hold fast the words 'The wisdom of God in a mystery ... God hath revealed them unto us by his Spirit.' As you gaze upon the cross, and long for conformity to him, be not weary or fearful because you cannot express in words what you seek. Ask him to plant the cross in your heart. Believe in him, the crucified and now living one, to dwell within you, and breathe his own mind there. Remember that his Holy Spirit, his crucifixion Spirit, is in you, not first of all to give you clear or beautiful thoughts, which might delude you, but to communicate the very temper and disposition out of which the cross grew. Accept your sense of ignorance heartily: depend entirely upon the Spirit to reveal the hidden mystery in 'the hidden part'; count confidently on the work he is doing in you. Keep your heart set on your crucified Lord

in meditation and worship, with an increasing sense of
how little you know or understand, and the blessed
Spirit will do his hidden work where you cannot see it.
Trust him fully: he will do it.

2. The cross is the wisdom of God in a mystery: the
Spirit of God alone can reveal it. How this would teach
us how to preach the cross aright. A mystery must be
accepted on authority. The apostle or preacher holds a
divine commission to tell men in the name of God what
they do not know, what they cannot understand, until
they first bow before God to accept it. The confidence
with which he speaks rests not on a message or a book
alone – that never alone can enable him to speak as one
who knows and witnesses. His commission is a living one
– in such measure as the Holy Spirit has revealed the
cross to him and in him, can he testify in power of what
it is and does. The mystery of God is, Christ in us, the
hope of glory – not a thought, but a life with its knowledge, not that of the mind, but of the renewed spirit.
The preacher can speak the mystery with authority,
when he knows that the office of God the Holy Spirit is
to give the mystery entrance into the heart however
dark. The word of divine authority and power brings
men into God's presence, wakens a sense of want and
desire, and inspires faith in an unseen but present
deliverance.

Is it any wonder that the preaching of the gospel is not
more effectual when men forget that they are preaching
a divine mystery to those whom the god of this world
hath blinded? The darkness of heart is a supernatural
one – the power that can enlighten is not the force of
reason or argument, not the persuasion of culture or
appeal, but the supernatural enlightening and quickening of the Holy Spirit. It is God 'who hath shined in our
hearts, to give the light of the knowledge of the glory of
God in the face of Jesus Christ.' The light of God shining
in the heart alone can witness to the mystery of his love
in the cross.

3. The cross the wisdom of God in a mystery: the Spirit

of God alone can reveal it. How the faith of this would make us fear the spirit of the world and its wisdom. The great hindrance to the preaching of the cross is a worldly spirit. And the worldly spirit proves itelf in nothing so much as in that which is its chief boast – its wisdom. There are only two possible ways of seeking to know the cross. The one is by the exercise of our natural powers, by the spirit of man, under the power of the spirit of the world; the other by the Spirit of God. The cross brings the message that everything in man is under the power of sin and the world, and that it is only through death to all that is of nature, that the life and the light of God can enter and prevail. Many speak and think of the Spirit of God as coming to dwell in and aid and use the natural spirit of men. This cannot be, until the spirit has bowed to the cross, has accepted its judgment, and has thus yielded itself to receive all from God. The preaching of the cross is the wisdom of man, expounding and defending and justifying and recommending it, and this can lead to nothing but making it of none effect. The spirit of the world, apparently honouring and proclaiming the cross, is the great cause why the church's preaching is so little in demonstration and in power. It robs the cross of what is its chief glory, that it is the wisdom of God in a mystery, with the Holy Spirit from heaven as its only interpreter.

The sense of mystery is of the very essence of true worship. Though at first it burdens and bows down, it soon becomes as the high mountain air, in which faith breathes free and strong. The sense of mystery brings the soul under the power of the invisible and eternal, the holy and divine. And the cross is the greatest of all mysteries – their sum and centre. In it we see the mystery of God – the Father ordaining, the Son bearing, the Spirit revealing and honouring it. The mystery of man – his sin, rejecting Christ; his curse, Christ forsaken of God; his worth, God's Son dying for him. The mystery of love – God offering himself to bear the sin and the suffering of man, and making man one with himself. The mystery of death and of life – death reigning, death conquered and made the gateway of life eternal. The mystery of redemption – the cross with its sin and shame made the power that conquers the sinner, and, while it humbles and slays, that wakens his hope and highest enthusiasm. The mystery of God's wisdom casting down reason and filling the heart with the light of God and eternity.

The cross the wisdom of God in a mystery: let us bow and worship and wait in deep humility. What God devised God will reveal. We are come to Mount Zion: the Lamb is the light thereof. As we adore what we cannot, would not understand, the Spirit will impart what God hath bestowed. And we shall learn to walk as men who know that what ear hath not heard, and what heart cannot conceive, God is working out in them that love him.

Chapter 4

The Preaching of the Cross and the Spirit

'O foolish Galatians ... before whose eyes Jesus Christ hath been evidently set forth, crucified among you, this only would I learn of you, Received ye the Spirit by the works of the law, or by the hearing of faith? ... Christ hath redeemed us from the curse of the law, being made a curse for us: for it is written, Cursed is every one that hangeth on a tree ... that we might receive the promise of the Spirit through faith.' Galatians 3:1–14

The cross and the Spirit are equally the power of God, but the cross is the hiding-place of that power, and, therefore, it is called the weakness of God and the foolishness of God. No man would have thought of seeking there for the power. Even the church understands little that there it must be found. The Spirit is the breaking forth of the power of God: when believers cry for it and wonder why they do not receive it, it can only be because they do not know its hiding-place. There may be a double mistake made. Some cling to the cross and know not the power they may wait for there, and some seek the power and know that at the cross it must be waited for. If the teaching of the church is to be full and fruitful, if it is to be the channel and the bearer of God's mighty saving power, it must, above everything, know and show the intimate union between the cross and the Spirit.

There is, perhaps, no part of holy Scripture where this is brought out so strikingly as in the epistle to the Galatians. Since the days of the Reformation the exposition of the doctrine of justification has been considered its chief object. The theme is a very much larger one. The apostle seeks to prove that not only justification, but the whole Christian life, with our continuance in the grace of Christ, is by faith. He reminds them that when Christ crucified had been set forth before them, they had, through faith, not only been justified, but received the Holy Spirit, and that it was only as they walked in the Spirit that salvation could truly be theirs.

One of the great causes of the feebleness of the Christian life is that men forget that conversion and justification are but the entrance to the way to heaven. The strait gate leads into the narrow way that leads to life: however great the importance of coming in by the right gate, the essential thing, and the only true proof that we are through the gate, is walking in the way to which it gave access. To speak of the epistle only or chiefly as teaching what justification is, may be the cause of a feeble life, in leading men to imagine that if the former be settled, the latter will follow of course. This is by no means the case. The epistle shows how believers need to be taught that the faith of the cross asks and leads to a life in the Spirit, and how through all time the preaching of the gospel means the message of the cross and the Spirit in their divine unity.

Let us begin by seeing what it teaches us of the cross. Here, too, we shall see how the power of the cross is by no means confined to atonement and justification on the entrance to the new life, but is in its inspiration and rule to characterise the whole life. We are to participate in all the cross and its death implies. Our share in the atonement of the cross is to be tested by our fellowship with it – our delight in sharing its disposition. There are four passages in the epistle referring to the cross, of special importance. One of these has reference to its atonement, three to its fellowship. The one is, 'Christ hath redeemed us from the curse of the law, being made a curse for us: for it is written, Cursed is every one that hangeth on a tree.' No words can teach more strongly that we have here, the doctrine of substitution. Here is the spotless, holy one, bearing a curse and a death that has not and could not be his own. And here the accursed become the redeemed from the curse. Here we have the tree, with its awful curse, as God's judgment on sin, attached to it. Christ was made sin – and why? For us, that we might become the righteousness of God in him. He was made a curse – and why? That his curse-bearing might be our ransom, and we be redeemed from the curse, free from it as he is free. The text deals with substitution and atonement. Christ is not only substitute, but also forerunner. He passed through the gate of death for us alone, that he might open a way for us now to walk with him. He could not have been substitute if he had not been our head, in perfect union with us. But as our head he not only died and lived for us, but comes with his death and life to live in us. He breathes his own crucifixion Spirit into us, and the cross which we learnt to know and trust as it stood there before us as our deliverance from the curse, becomes a power within us that delivers from the power of sin. There are three passages in the epistle in which this is expressed: 'I am crucified with Christ: nevertheless I live; yet not I, but Christ liveth in me.' 'They that are Christ's have crucified the flesh with the affections and lusts.' 'But God forbid that I should glory, save in the cross of our Lord Jesus Christ, by whom the world is crucified unto me, and I unto the world.' Here the one thought is, the living vital union with Christ, by which we can say Christ the crucified lives in me. I have been crucified with him; I have in his power and likeness crucified the flesh on his cross; through the cross the world is crucified to me, and I to the world. The cross is God's judgment on sin. God has condemned the flesh and the world to the cross: in union with Christ I have accepted the sentence, and in the power of Christ's life I live as one crucified with him, with the disposition and the spirit of the cross as the mark of my discipleship.

It is easy to see what the result must be of the exclusive presentation of the atonement as the one object of God's teaching and our acceptance of the cross. Men are led to regard pardon as the one thing needful, and the actual imitation and following of the crucified Lord is neglected. Were the teaching of the epistle understood and accepted, men would see how the cross that won our pardon wins our heart and life too. The soul that begins to live the cross would count this its highest honour to be crucified with Christ on it, to live daily in the inner spiritual crucifixion fellowship with him, delivered from the power of the flesh and the world as the two great powers of sin condemned of God to the cross as accursed. The cross would, indeed, become in daily life the power of God.

Let us now see how with the teaching on the cross there is combined the teaching on the Spirit. How clear it is in our text, 'Christ hath been evidently set forth, crucified among you' (Gal 3:1). With what result? Through this preaching of Christ crucified and faith in him 'Received ye the Spirit' (Gal 3:2). And then, farther on, 'Christ redeemed us from the curse, being made a curse for us, for it is written, Cursed is every one that hangeth on a tree (Gal 3:12), that we might receive the promise of the Spirit through faith (Gal 3:14). The redemption of the cross leads to the reception of the Spirit. In chapter 4, we have the same order: 'God sent forth his Son ... To redeem them that were under the law, that we might receive the adoption of Sons', as the fruit of the redemption. 'And because ye are Sons, God hath sent forth the Spirit of his Son into your hearts.' The redemption of Christ always leads to the indwelling of the Spirit. See it again in the very remarkable passage, Galatians 5:16–26, where the work of the Spirit is clearly set forth as the only power of a holy life. On the mention of what the fruit of the Spirit is, there follows at once, as if in answer to the question, How does the Spirit bring forth all this fruit? What of the flesh? 'They that are Christ's have crucified the flesh with the affections and lusts.' And on this again, 'If we live in the Spirit, let us also walk in the Spirit.' Between two deeply significant texts on the Spirit comes in this of the flesh crucified. The knowledge of the cross and the Spirit together is the only power for the daily life of holiness.

It is the glory of Pentecost that it was the full consummation of Christ's work, the actual restoration of what had been lost in paradise. Man, who had been created in God's image for his fellowship and indwelling, had, in doing his own will, and yielding to the self life, lost his God. The death of the cross affected the death of the self life, and won for us the life of God. 'The communication of the Holy Spirit is nothing but God taking possession of us.' Let us accept the cross in the faith that it has secured for us, will bring us to, will keep us in, a life filled with the Spirit. Let us accept the Spirit in the longing desire and the perfect confidence that he will lead us into the perfect experience of all conformity to Christ the cross is meant to work in us. We all admit the truth: without the cross there never could have been a coming of the Spirit. Let us hold with equal firmness the truth that follows from it: without the cross having full mastery of our life there is no fullness of the Spirit. When God set before his Son the cross, he steadfastly set his face towards it. Crucifixion by the world, and to the world, the crucifixion of human nature with all that is counted dear and precious, its very will and love of life, death to everything of earth and human hope, for the sake of an entirely new life to be received from God in heaven out of death – this was the Spirit that was in Jesus on earth, of which the Spirit at Pentecost was the communication. This Spirit of our Lord on earth, this is what the church must seek above everything, if she is to be clothed with power from above.

Let us ask God to teach us to live as men who know how the cross and the Spirit are linked. Let us pray to him to give us preachers who set forth Christ crucified both as the Redeemer from the curse, and the Deliverer from the power of sin, and teach us to love the cross much as we see Christ dying for us; but still more as it unites us closer to him in our dying with him. Let us yield ourselves to the indwelling of the Spirit, that is, of Christ crucified come again in the Spirit to dwell in our hearts, that our whole life in the world, in body, soul and spirit, may prove that the cross we glory in is nothing but the cross of our Lord Jesus through which the world is crucified to us, and we to the world.

Chapter 5

Nothing but the Cross

'I came not with excellency of speech or of wisdom, declaring unto you the testimony of God. For I determined not to know anything among you, save Jesus Christ, and him crucified.' 1 Corinthians 2:1–2

How often this text has been taken for a minister's first sermon. And how often the chief thought has been that the atoning work of Christ on the cross is the sum and substance of the gospel – the only ground of a sinner's hope. The text does indeed mean this; but it means a great deal more. It is not alone the work of Christ but the living Christ himself, as the crucified one, that the gospel reveals. A sinner often wearies himself in vain in trying to take hold of the work of Christ and its blessings. When he sees that it is Jesus Christ himself, and him crucified, he has to trust, he finds one who takes charge and works all in him.

And very often the text has been also used as if we read, not to preach 'anything but Jesus Christ and him crucified.' The word not to know anything means a very great deal more. It says, 'not to know', either in what I preach, or in the spirit of my preaching and living, anything but a crucified Lord. That it refers to the spirit of the preaching, as well as the contents, is proved by the little word 'for'. 'I came not with excellency of speech or of wisdom, for', to have done so, even though I preached the cross, would have been inconsistent with my determination not to know anything; not to be, or allow, or indulge in anything that was not in perfect harmony with the spirit and the life of Jesus Christ and him crucified.

This deeper meaning of the word know, in connection with the spiritual life, runs through all Scripture. We find it specially with St John and St Paul. When the latter says, 'I count all things but loss for the excellency of the knowledge of Christ Jesus my Lord,' he immediately gives us the interpretation, 'That I may know him, and the power of his resurrection, and the fellowship of his sufferings, being made conformable unto his death.' Just as I cannot by any possibility know the taste or nourishing power of a food, except by partaking of it, so there is no way of knowing Christ Jesus and him crucified, but by receiving him into my life, and being made partaker of the disposition that animated his life and his cross. Jesus Christ is the revelation of the life of God, as it appears and acts in human nature. In the Holy Spirit, Jesus Christ is come from heaven to live and act in his disciples. We only know Jesus Christ as far as we partake of his nature and life and spirit.

In that life of our Lord the most remarkable thing, its great feature, its divine mystery and glory, was his being crucified on the cross. He proved how life has no object but as it can be made to serve God's will; how suffering and sacrificing all is the highest and most well-pleasing religion and obedience; how there is no way out of the life into which he has brought us into the glory of God, but through dying to it. The determination not to know anything save Jesus Christ and him crucified, means the purpose to sacrifice everything, to obtain as complete a conformity to Jesus, in his crucifixion spirit, as possible. It was this that made Paul what he was: the crucified Christ was not only his surety and his Saviour, but the only model and measure of what his life was to be. 'I came to you not with excellency of speech', as little as Christ sought after it, might I do so, 'for I determined not to know anything among you, save Jesus Christ and him crucified.' As in preaching, so in living; as in the truth I taught about him, so in my whole disposition and behaviour; I was determined you should see nothing but Christ crucified.

To the church of Christ has been committed the sacred trust of lifting up his cross in the world, and honouring it, preaching it, specially bearing and living it, and so exhibiting its attractiveness and power. It is as the church proves that there is something in the cross that is so heavenly and blessed that everything is gladly sacrificed to it, that men will believe in it; not as for atonement, but as the most perfect expression of the most perfect life. It is as the church proves itself the very body of the Lord Jesus, by showing forth the very same life there was in him, that his power as head can freely flow through her. It is as her determination not to know anything but Jesus Christ and him crucified is seen in her being crucified with Christ, being crucified to the world, that his resurrection, joy and power can be manifested in her. In the church the world must hear and see Christ Jesus and him crucified.

If such is the calling of the church, it can only be realised through her individual members, and first of all through her leaders, those who are specially set apart as the messengers of the cross. Such intense devotion to the cross and the crucified Lord, as works inward and outward conformity to him, is the first requisite of the gospel minister, if Paul is at all to be counted a model for imitation. It was the one secret of his ministry and his power.

Well might St Paul say, 'I determined not to know anything among you, save Christ, and him crucified.' Had it not been for this determination, he had never known what he knew, when he said, 'The life that I now live is not mine, but Chrit's that liveth in me.' For as Christ's, intending nothing, knowing nothing, willing nothing, but purely and solely the whole course of his crucifying process, was the whole truth of his being come in the flesh, was his doing the whole will of him that sent him, was his overcoming the world, death, and hell, so he that embraces this process, as Christ embraced it, who is wholly given up to it, as Christ was, he has the will of Christ, he has the mind of Christ, and may therefore well desire to know nothing else. 'Is this man alone? Is the world, death, and hell known to be overcome in him, as they were in Christ?'

It was in and through this crucifixion spirit that Christ's saving power was revealed. That spirit and that power was revealed. That spirit and that power dwelt in him as a disposition, a life principle, manifesting itself to his disciples and all who came into contact with him. Now he is in heaven, his saving power acts in no other way as a life-principle taking possession of his saints and working through them. And when the church has to complain about witholding the saving power, the reason must be that the crucifixion spirit, in which the saving power finds its life, is lacking. It must be because the church is not saying as Paul said, 'I came not with excellency of speech or of wisdom, declaring unto you the testimony of God, for I determined not to know anything save Jesus Christ, and him crucified.'

We must ever return to our Lord, and men like his servant Paul, and see what the elements are that go to make up the crucifixion spirit. A deep sense of the sinfulness of sin, and of the righteousness of God's judgment on it; an entire separation from the world, and a clear protest against its apostasy from God, under the power of the god of this world: a life-long surrender to our own will and pleasure as a sacrifice to God to work out his will in us; a parting with all excellency of speech and wisdom as making the cross of none effect; a passion of love for the souls of men, giving its life as completely up for them as Christ did; the acceptance of death to all that is of human nature as sinful and under the curse that the life and power of heaven may work all in us: this was the spirit that animated Paul as it had animated Jesus Christ. This was the spirit in which he said, 'I bear in my body the marks of the Lord Jesus.' This is the spirit that must still animate the church. The spirit of Christ that led him to the cross, that flows out to us through the cross, that reveals and glorifies the cross – this must be the spirit in which the church lives, and suffers, and influences if it is to bless the world.

'I count all things loss except for the excellency of the knowledge of Christ Jesus my Lord ... That I may know him ... being made conformable unto his death.' The cross means the sacrifice of all. To know the crucified in the conformity of his death, we need to count all things loss. The cross demands the life. It is a ministry that comes not in excellency of speech, or wisdom, but boasts in the 'weakness' and the 'foolishness' of the cross that will convict the world of its sin and its earthliness, and will lift men up to a supernatural life. The cross brings to each one who believes in it, the death that is 'the gate of life.' There is given through it the fullness and the power of the Spirit.

Chapter 6

The Cross Made of None Effect

'Christ sent me ... to preach the gospel: not with wisdom of words, lest the cross of Christ should be made of none effect.'
1 Corinthians 1:17

What a solemn thought that the cross of Christ can be made of none effect! That people may love to hear of it, may bring it, as they think, their homage of reverence and trust, and yet in their lives prove that it has none effect! It has no power over them to bring them into the death that is the gate of the true life.

And what a solemn thought that it is not by great sin, or unbelief, or enmity that this comes, but simply – by the wisdom of words. The spirit of the world seeks to accept and adorn the cross, so as to make it attractive to men, and so – it makes it of none effect!

And what a solemn thought that just the very messengers of the cross, the men to whom Christ entrusted the preaching of it, should be guilty of this folly – spending their lives in preaching the cross, and all the while making it of none effect! Even Paul was in danger of doing this. And so Christ, when he sent him to preach the gospel, gave him just this one warning: not with wisdom of words, lest the cross of Christ should be made of none effect!

And, once more, what a solemn thought that this may be done all unconsciously, and that, while men are wondering and discussing why the preaching of the cross has not more power, the answer that is nearest is not thought of: It is the wisdom of words makes it of none effect.

And, saddest of all, what a solemn thought that the church, in the way she trains her ministers, in the undue prominence given in study and education to culture and literature, may be actually fitting men most effectively to do the work that makes the cross they preach powerless – training them in wisdom of words!

Would God that ears and hearts may be opened to hear the voice from heaven to all who preach the gospel: not with wisdom of words, lest the cross of Christ should be made of none effect.

It is often said in regard to preaching that the essential thing is the subjectmatter, and that thus our one care should be to see that what we preach is God's truth. However much this view may appear to honour the Word, it is far from correct. To know how to preach is of as vital importance as to know what to preach. Paul might have preached the truth of the cross – if he had not done so in the right way, without wisdom of words, he would have made it of none effect. Thousands have preached the cross to little purpose, because there was something wanting in the spirit in which they did it. In time of danger a man may make a patriotic speech with the matter admirable and the arguments unanswerable. The truth he speaks must be truth to him and in him; it is the spirit and life that there is in him that gives his words their weight. What we preach – that has reference to Christ and his work for us on the cross. How we preach – that points to the Holy Spirit and his work in us through the cross. To both our preaching must render equal honour if it is to be effectual. It is not the doctrinal correctness of the truth, but the very truth of God living in us, that works preaching in demonstration of the Spirit and of power.

Paul's commission was thus: Beware of preaching anything but the cross as your gospel; beware of preaching in any other but its own spirit.

And what was the mark of that other spirit that was to be avoided? Throughout the first three chapters of this first epistle to the Corinthians, there is one clear answer given, with the little word not continually repeated: Not with wisdom of words; not the wisdom of the wise; not the wisdom of this world; not with excellency of speech or wisdom; not with enticing words of man's wisdom; not the wisdom of men; not the wisdom of the princes of this world; not in words which men's wisdom preacheth, but in words which the Holy Spirit teacheth. If any man among you seemeth to be wise in this world, let him become a fool that he may be wise, for the wisdom of the world is foolishness with God, because the foolishness of God is wiser than men. The kingdom of God is not in word, but in power. Let us read and take in these words of the Holy Spirit until we see how the one great temptation the preacher of the cross has to fear, the one great power by which satan makes that preaching of none effect, is – words of man's wisdom.

All this is the opposite of what we hear in our days. We are asked whether the mind is not indeed one of God's most wondrous gifts, indispensable to knowing him; and whether he and his service ought not to have the best we can give. 'The highest existence in the universe,' it is said, 'is mind, for God is mind, and the development of that principle which assimilates to God must be our supreme good.' Men forget or ignore what Scripture says about the mind being carnal, corrupt, blinded, so that it is only as the believer is transformed in the progressive renewing of his mind that he can know spiritual things. We are taught that the gospel must be adapted to the age by translation; that this can only be done when the preacher is in full sympathy with the aspirations and tendencies of the time; and that we must cast into the fair moulds which we owe to men of genius the message of heavenly peace.

Men do not see that as the student throws himself heart and soul into the literature of the age to enter fully into its tendencies and aspirations, and to acquire the power of re-casting the message of peace into the fair forms that please men, he comes himself under its power. The kingdom of this world, even as the kingdom of heaven, refuses to unlock its treasure on any condition but that of enthusiastic devotion. And however staunchly orthodox the preacher may remain in proclaiming the atonement of the cross, the desire of meeting the men of the world halfway, and gratifying their taste, will rob the preaching of its power. And gradually the cross will become in the preaching what it has become in act – the symbol of certain truths with regard to suffering and love which the world can admire, while God's thoughts as to the necessity and effect of that suffering, the enmity and curse of man's sin, and the object and claims of that love, in atonement and a supernatural redemption, are rejected.

If once we are willing to accept the divine message 'not with wisdom of words,' it will not be difficult to find the reason for the prohibition. Think of the devotion of time and the intense concentration of effort needed to acquire the wisdom of man – to how many it has been the loss of their spiritual fervour? What we spend so much time and labour on we cannot but value – how natural it is, all unconsciously, to put our trust in it – a trust that leads us away from that entire dependence upon God and his Spirit which alone has the promise of power. Think of the difficulty of preaching the true cross – God's cross – man's estimate and rejection of Christ, God's revelation of sin and his curse on it, and his redemption for the guilty, the crucifixion of the believer to the world, and of the world to him, in a way to gratify the literary taste or the worldly prejudice of those who are called the educated. It is an impossibility. The only result must be – making the cross of none effect.

No; Christ's method was a different one. He came with a message that caused offence to human wisdom, even among his own disciples. At Pentecost his disciples took up the position of bold and uncompromising antagonism to the world. Paul gloried in a cross that was a stumbling-block and foolishness: the very thought of the offence of the cross ceasing was to him a sign of compromise with the flesh. The foolishness of preaching, the foolishness of a crucified Christ, the foolishness of God – these are, for all ages, as long as the world is the world, the only power that is to be wiser and stronger than men. Instead of deluding men with the idea that the worldly mind can be coaxed or argued into the acceptance of the cross, the gospel comes boldly to preach a cross which is to show men the innate enmity of their heart against God, and the depth of their misery under his curse. Hide this from men, or soften it down – they may accept of the cross and Christ who died upon it; it cannot be to them the power of God to salvation; they will never learn through it to die to sin and self and the world, or to glory in it because it crucifies them to the world. It is easy for man's wisdom to win men to a cross that leaves them uncrucified. True gospel preaching is to be led by God's wisdom to offer the cross with all its sin and guilt, with all its exacting demand of unconditional surrender and crucifixion with Christ, and then to trust to God's power to give that which appears foolishness and a stumbling-block acceptance and victory.

The cross came not by man or man's wisdom. In opposition to all man's wisdom it was God's wisdom revealed on earth. Even so now, it is the opposite of man's wisdom that will convert and save. If God's servants will but seek to know that which human wisdom cannot give them, which it will most surely hide from them – what God's thoughts are of the cross, and how his power works in its foolishness and weakness, they will learn to believe in its sufficiency to break its own way into the heart, to humble and to lead, to slay and make alive again. They will discover what has been the reason that the preaching of the cross has comparatively so little effect, and, in casting aside human wisdom, they will see, as never before, the need of being led by God himself into the mysteries of the cross through a life crucified with Christ. Their preaching of the power of the cross will become the utterance of their heart – experience – a testimony to God's power in them, a proof of God's power through them.

Chapter 7

The Crucifixion of the Flesh

'They that are Christ's have crucified the flesh with the affections and lusts.' Galatians 5:24

'They that are Christ's have crucified the flesh.' It is not, must crucify; not, do crucify; not, seek to crucify. No, but, have crucified: it is a finished transaction. And it is not, they who are wholly Christ's and fully follow him; not, they who are advanced in the Christian life, truly spiritual people. No, the statement is universal: They that are of Christ Jesus, all who have believed in him, the weakest and the youngest, have crucified the flesh. What does this mean?

When a man enters through a gate into a long path on which he undertakes to walk to reach a certain aim, he does not yet know all its difficulties and trials, but if he has honestly, after hearing what has been told him, and counting the cost, committed himself to that path, we consider him to have accepted all that may come. Even so the believer, when he accepted the crucified Christ as his Saviour, accepted that path of the cross to which Christ has bound each of his disciples. He may know but little of what it implies, but he has yielded himself to all that believing in and following a crucified Saviour implies. And he will find one of the first things Scripture and the Holy Spirit teach him, that just as the atonement of the cross sets the gate open and faith in it enters in, so the fellowship of the cross is itself the new and living way in which he has to walk. Just as faith in Christ crucified for me is my first step, so Christ crucified living in me, my being crucified with Christ and like Christ is the mark and power of the life I now live by faith. 'They that are Christ's,' they were all in him when he was crucified; they have all set their seal to it when they accepted him, though they could not yet fully understand that the flesh, as sinful, deserves the curse, has been condemned to the cross in Christ; that all that is flesh must die. In Christ all flesh, their flesh too was crucified: in accepting him, 'they have crucified the flesh with the affections and lusts.'

Many believers do not know this. They neither know that the flesh needs to be crucified, nor that they have given their consent, and adjudged their flesh to the cross. The church is suffering inconceivable harm from its ignorance of, or silence regarding, this truth. The cross of Jesus as the crucifixion of our flesh needs to be preached again. Nothing less can give the cross the honour and the place it claims; nothing less can bring deliverance from the power of the world and sin.

And what is this flesh which we are here taught we have crucified? Generally speaking, it means our fallen human nature, as it is under the power of sin. It manifests itself, first of all, in what are called the sins of the flesh, as the flesh seeks its gratification through the body and its appetites. Thus Paul begins and ends his summing up of the works of the flesh with 'adultery, fornication, uncleanness, lasciviousness ... drunkenness, revellings, and such like.' He then includes with these sins of the body, those of the soul – 'idolatry, witchcraft, hatred, variance, emulations, wrath, strife, seditions, heresies, envyings, murders.'

But even this is not all. There is a religion of the flesh which is just as far from God as the sins of the flesh. He warns the Galatians of those who preach circumcision and do away with the offence of the cross, as those who 'make a fair shew in the flesh,' who 'glory in the flesh' instead of 'in the cross of our Lord Jesus Christ.'

There is a religious flesh as well as a sinful flesh. There is a carnal mind, the mind of the flesh, which in its own wisdom thinks it knows the way to serve God. There is a carnal zeal, which is very diligent in striving to carry out its own thought of New Testament religion, without waiting for the teaching of God's Spirit. There is a carnal will, the will of the flesh, which with its resolves and efforts does its utmost to live a holy life, or to do God's work, and wonders at its bad success. The reason is, very simply, that it is the attempt to do in man's wisdom and man's power what the Spirit of God alone can do. All that is of the flesh is equally rejected by God: all that is flesh has been crucified in Christ to make way for the new life of the Spirit. Of all that he does or strives to do in his own will the believer must be brought to accept the teaching: they that are of Christ have crucified the flesh, with all its affections and desires, all the power of human nature and of self dwelling in it. All the worship and service of God is to be wholly in the Spirit.

It is the great need of the church of our day to have this crucifixion of the flesh preached, and the cross of Christ restored to its place. It is to be feared that with all our striving after culture and taste and eloquence and power in preaching, with all our talk of bright and attractive services, with all our efforts to win on the one hand the cultivated higher classes, and on the other the lapsed masses, to our churches, we are putting our confidence in the flesh, and preparing for ourselves bitter disappointment. The cross is the power of God: they that are Christ's must prove in preaching and living that they have crucified the flesh: it is the cross alone that can give the victory.

But if this is to be, then believers will need to prove in their life that they have indeed crucified and so are able to conquer the passions and lusts of the flesh, whether in the life of the soul or the body. As long as Christians do not prove that all sins against the law of love, hatred and variance, wrath and strife and envying have been crucified, and as such have no dominion, the preaching of the cross, the warfare against a carnal religion, or against the carnal life of worldly men, will avail little. Before he went to the cross, and thence to heaven, Christ prepared for himself a little band of men and women who followed him to death, bearing their cross after him. Them he sent in the power of the Spirit to preach the cross. A church in which such ministers and believers are found will have power with God and men.

The victory over sin against the law of love, all pride, temper, envy, selfishness; the fruit of the Spirit – love, joy, peace, longsuffering, gentleness – cannot come from the flesh; no struggling or effort can gain them. They only come to the crucified; to men who yield themselves to the Holy Spirit that he may make their crucifixion with Christ truth and power.

And in no other way can the deliverance from the lowest form of lusts of the flesh be obtained. Christ bore our sins in his body on the tree: He hath reconciled you in the body of his flesh to present you holy and without blemish before him. It is in the body too that the power of his crucifixion and redemption can be known. It is doubtful whether Christians know to what extent the gratification of the body, say, in eating and drinking for pleasure, may interrupt or make impossible that unbroken communion with God they desire. While we think we are only feeding the body we may be feeding and strengthening that flesh or self which gains power by every indulgence. To maintain the crucifixion of the flesh every moment – and that is what is absolutely need-ful if it be true that in our flesh dwelleth no good thing – is what cannot be done in our power. But the Holy Spirit, when he shows us the heavenly blessedness of the likeness to Christ, can give us the will and the heart and the courage for it. All our modern ideas of what is need-ful for comfort or pleasure are the product of the spirit of the world. We have been born and bred in the midst of it, and are hardly conscious of how far all its ease and indulgence in daily life enervates our will, and makes us incapable of that true spirituality which is the fruit of the unbroken presence and rule of the Spirit.

Saints in all ages have complained of the power of evil in their hearts, suggesting thoughts and feelings from which they revolted; they came involuntarily, and were utterly beyond their control – the motions of sin in their members, fleshly lusts which war against the soul. It is well to remember that these are more closely connected with the state of the body than we think, and that, though not to be directly controlled by an act of the will, they can be met by that which is in the power of the will, the temperance and abstinence which keeps the body under. The danger of free and full eating lies not only in its unfitting for direct fellowship with God, but in the stimulus it gives to the flesh in other directions. What indulges and nourishes it on one side, strengthens it as a whole. Nothing can give deliverance, but in everything and always walk in the faith of our having yielded up all that is of the flesh to the crucifixion of Christ.

'They that are Christ's have crucified the flesh with the affections and lusts.' To know how the power of this life can be formed and maintained, notice the context. The words lie imbedded in the passage on the work of the Spirit. They are preceded by the injunction, 'Walk in the Spirit, and ye shall not fulfil the lust of the flesh,' with the description of the works of the flesh and the fruit of the Spirit. And then followed by the renewed injunc-tion: 'If we live in the Spirit, let us also walk in the Spirit.' This being crucified with Christ, which includes the 'have crucified the flesh,' is a part of that life in Christ which the Spirit has brought us, and which he alone can apply and carry on. All our attempts to crucify the flesh, or to keep it crucified, are vain: we need the light and joy of the Holy Spirit to show us what is ours in Christ, what has been given in our union with him, and what he himself will make true in our experience. The very thought of having to keep the flesh crucified may be, very often is, as of a burden, and a strain, and an impossibility: the knowledge and acceptance and faith of the indwelling Spirit makes it part of the great salvation God effectually works out in us.

Believer, you have the Spirit of the living God dwelling in you. All we tell you of the cross and the crucified life and the crucifixion of the flesh is not to tell you what you are to do, but what you may confidently expect the Holy Spirit to do in you. It is to show you what his work is, that you may in deep humility and entire dependence, but also with joyous faith, claim and receive it. Do begin, at once, to believe, to praise God, to rejoice that you can do nothing but through the Spirit, that you are sure that you can do all things through Christ's Spirit strengthening you.

Chapter 8

Bearing the Cross

'*He that taketh not his cross, and followeth after me, is not worthy of me. He that findeth his life shall lose it: and he that loseth his life for my sake shall find it.*' Matthew 10:38–39

Our blessed Lord twice spoke to his disciples of taking up the cross as the condition of their being his followers. The first time in his charge here which he gave to his disciples on first sending them out; he said that anyone who did not take up his cross was not worthy of him. The second time, when, after he had given the first intimation of his death, Peter had rebuked him, and been in his turn rebuked, he taught them how not only he, but they too, would equally have to choose the cross. On each occasion he added the significant words about losing life for his sake, as the only way of finding it. The cross is the only path, death the only gate, of life.

It is difficult for us to conceive how strange and

altogether unintelligible the expression 'taking up the cross' must have appeared to the disciples. The sound of the words has become so familiar to us that they make but little impression; bearing the cross has become a proverb. In the time of Christ there was no such proverb; the cross was, as the gallows with us, nothing but the symbol of a shameful death. It was much as if a teacher in our days were to invite his disciples to take a gallows as their badge. The cross was the punishment for slaves, for the worst malefactors, for the most hated enemies. And Christ says that except a man take up his cross, he is not worthy of him. He had nowhere as yet spoken of his own death on the cross. But the words he adds could leave no doubt as to his meaning something very real and solemn; he that findeth (loveth, saveth) his life, shall lose it: he that loseth his life for my sake, shall find it. Taking up the cross could mean nothing else but the preparation to be crucified, to die, to lose one's life.

How little the disciples were able to understand the word. And still less were they prepared to accept it with all it implied. But Christ gave them the word as a seed-thought; in the course of his teaching and suffering they would gradually find the exposition of the wonderous text he had given them, and then, in the coming of the Holy Spirit, the blessed power to enter into the full fellowship of his cross. The word 'taking the cross' is still now, as then, one of deep mystery, which only the teaching of Christ himself as we follow him, and the power of the eternal Spirit through whom he bore the cross, can reveal within us as an actual losing of our life. What the disciples could not understand from its strangeness, we fail to apprehend from its familiarity. Every man must bear his cross; the thought is so common in reference to the most ordinary trials or crosses of life, both with those who do not know Christ, that the deep meaning of Christ's word is often entirely lost. We need to go back to himself, and take the word, as he spake it first, afresh again as a seed-thought into our hearts; as we seek truly and fully to do, what he couples with it, to follow him, he

will open up in our heart all the meaning and power of
the sacred mystery.

Blessed Lord, do thou in every deed breathe by your
Holy Spirit the words as a power and a life through our
whole being: 'He that doth not take his cross, and follow
after me, is not worthy of me. He that loseth his life for
my sake, shall find it.' Fill us with a deep, deep longing
to know thy full meaning, and to live worthy of thee.

'Take his cross and follow me.' – The bearing of the
cross and the following of Christ are inseparable. It is
only the cross-bearer who is accepted as a follower: it is
only in following Christ that we find the path and the
power in which to bear the cross. The call to follow him
was the earlier and apparently the simpler; the demand
to take up the cross was only the unfolding of what the
following included. The full apprehension of what following Christ means will wonderfully help to know what
bearing the cross implies. When Jesus called the twelve
to forsake all and follow him, it meant giving up all, not
only their property and occupations, but their whole way
of living and thinking, to live and think, to act, and be,
in everything like him. They did not understand this at
first; their call at first was more external; its meaning was
only by degrees opened up. But as he led them on step by
step, they gradually were led to see that they had to follow him in paths they never had dreamt of, even to the
drinking of his cup, and the being baptised with his baptism, to the humiliation that made him the servant of all,
ready to give his life as a ransom for many. When he
spoke of taking up the cross it was only the unfolding of
what the following had all along been aiming it.

Even so with us, too, the call 'Follow me', is often very
heartily accepted and obeyed by those who have but
little idea of what it is going to lead to. There are certain
paths of conduct and duty in which Christ is seen to lead;
there are certain tempers and dispositions in which his
example is acknowledged to be binding; but there is very
little thought of his demand being that we are indeed to
take him and his life as our exact model. And still less it

is seen that we have not only to take him entirely as our pattern, trying as far as possible to be conformed to him, but that we are to see and get rid of the whole of our own life, and to have his very life and spirit and power working in us. It is when this, the true and full meaning of following Christ, dawns upon us, that we begin to see how taking our cross is the most essential part of it. The whole life and work of Christ would have been in vain had he not taken his cross. The cross was the one aim and object of his life; on the cross he finished his work and won his victory; his cross is his glory. And how could he hold out to men the privilege of following him and having fellowship with him, and exclude them from the very best and the most indispensable, that which is the entrance to the life and the glory of heaven. No, taking the cross and following Christ are inseparable. He that would truly walk in fellowship with Christ, as a true and full follower, must share in Christ's love for the cross, and rejoice to bear it.

And what did Christ's taking the cross mean? He saw that death was the only path through which, as the Redeemer of our human nature, he could reach God and bring us there; the cross was to him the end of our old man, his entrance and our entrance with him to new life. And so when we see that to be crucified with Christ is our privilege, and that to enter fully into that is our only route into the full experience of the resurrection life, and that accepting, taking our cross. Christ's cross, as ours, is our blessed path to the full conformity to Christ's death, we understand how of all that is included in following Christ the taking the cross is the very centre. And every longing for likeness to Christ brings us back to the one prayer: The partnership of thy cross, Lord, make me worthy of it, and reveal it in me.

In regard to this following of Christ there is one thing that is not sufficiently noted. It is not, in the gospel, a command to all who seek salvation from Christ, but a special call to the inner circle of those who were to go with him in his ministry, to be trained for his service: 'If any man serve me, let him follow me.' It was to this inner circle that the word was always spoken by Christ. This teaches us the solemn and blessed lesson that they who would truly be Christ's servants, and be taught of him to teach others, must follow him in a very special sense. And that this special following will be nothing but a very special conformity to him in his cross-bearing. In the church of our day we have still the two circles: those who are specially set apart to the ministry of the word, and those who are to serve God in the ordinary vocations of life. Alas, the distinction has largely become an external instead of a spiritual one. Gifts, and learning, and training, and human ordination have had too much to do with it. As the spirit of Christ moves more mightily in his church, they who follow Christ most closely in his humility, and meekness, they who know best to bear the cross, and breath most of the spirit of their crucified Lord, will be recognised as the first in the kingdom of heaven. The cross will be the one badge of the followers of Christ.

We thank God that Christ is no longer on earth, so that the privilege of following him and being trained by himself must be confined to a select few. There is a spiritual ministry to which access is open to all. Its mark is the following of the crucified One. Its spirit is the crucifixion spirit. Its glory is the cross whereby it is crucified to the world, to the flesh, to self with all its will and honour. In the cross, in the conscious weakness, and in the foolishness which it is in the sight of men, it finds the wisdom of God and the power of God. It counts all things but loss to know Christ, and to be made conformable to his death. None but Christ himself can give entrance to its service; nothing but the cross, with its death to the old self, and its admission to the full life of God, makes the disciple worthy of him.

The person who does not take up his cross, and follow me, is not worthy of me! How little the disciples understood the mystery of the cross, as they had to bear it! But Jesus took them, in their ignorant but honest and wholehearted surrender to follow him, and led them, by a way that they know not, to Calvary and the grave. He taught them, not by words, but in his own fellowship, what it meant. How little we understand the mystery of the cross, as we are to bear it! But our blessed Lord will teach us. Let us make it the watchword of our life: take thy cross and follow me. Be our one desire, a life as completely devoted to the Father as his was; a life, in death to the world and self, wholly given up to God and our fellows. We shall prove, for ourselves and for others, the cross is the power of God!

Chapter 9

The Cross the Test of Discipleship

'*He that taketh not his cross, and followeth after me, is not worthy of me.*' Matthew 10:38

'*If any man will come after me, let him deny himself, and take up his cross, and follow me.*' Matthew 16:24

'*Whosoever doth not bear his cross, and come after me, cannot be my disciple.*' Luke 14:27

On three different occasions our Lord spoke of his disciples bearing his cross. The first was in his ordination charge to preach. The form in which the truth was put was: 'He that taketh not his cross … is not worthy of me.' The second time the word was addressed to the Twelve at Caesarea Philippi, when he had spoken of his sufferings and been rebuked by Peter. Here he said: 'If any man come after me ... let him take up his cross.' The third time the word was spoken to the great multitude following him: 'Whosoever doth not bear his cross, and come after me, cannot be my disciple.'

These words are almost always used as applicable to all Christians. And yet this is not their first meaning. The word 'disciple' (learners) is used in a double sense. It is sometimes applied to all who believed in Christ, accepting him as their Teacher and Lord. More frequently it refers to those who literally left their homes and goods to follow him from place to place, and specially of the Twelve. When our Lord speaks of coming after him, of following him, it is this inner circle of which he thinks. It was not in Christ's mind the question of salvation, but of external discipleship. Many who never came after him, who never forsook all to follow him, found life and salvation in him. Christ chose for himself a company of men whom he was to train to take over his work when he left the world. To these, others, as the women who followed him, joined themselves. And it is of such Christ says: Whosoever does not come after me literally, and bear his cross, cannot be my disciple, is not worthy of me.

The more direct application to the literal and external following of Christ by no means takes away or weakens the general principle as the law of all Christ's followers. The more limited application gives emphasis to the great truth that Christ wants some among his disciples to be the special partners and representatives of his cross-bearing. He wanted those who were to have the high privilege of being prepared by himself for continuing his work on earth, when he left for heaven, to understand that, as the cross was the consummation and full revelation of his work, so his chosen messengers were above everything to be like him in bearing their cross; they were to carry the cross in their life as well as preach it. It is of great importance that we should see how there is still need and room in the church for this twofold application of the words. There are Christians who are called by God to take their part in the political and social questions of the day. There are others who feel that their calling lies in a different direction, that all the time and strength they have must go to directly spiritual work, the cultivation of the life of faith and prayer in themselves and others. Until this diversity of gift and calling is understood there will always be division and mutual condemnation. One says: Every true Christian ought to take part in the politics of his country. Another maintains: No true Christian can or may do so. Both are equally wrong. The law of the spirit of life in Christ Jesus is the law of liberty. It is only as this is acknowledged that the unity of the body of Christ can be maintained in love amidst the external diversity. It is only then that all will learn that none of the members of the body have their powers or functions on their own behalf. He that is free for an entirely spiritual life and work is so only that what he gathers from heaven may be for the benefit of his brethren who have not received from God the same capacity or calling. And he who as a Christian feels himself called to take part in the strife of politics, must know that the prayer and the love of his brethren who do not enter with him into the field of conflict are bringing him strength and blessing.

The principle on which all this rests is what we see everywhere. It is what is expressed by the modern word specialism. Men devote themselves in science or business to some one particular branch. That devotion neither proves contempt for other pursuits, nor asserts the superiority or sufficiency of that which the specialist has adopted. All he does will be contributed to the general welfare. The solidarity of the race, the unity of a nation, is as real as that of the human body; the members exist and act for the welfare of each other. Even the head, though ruling all the members, is limited to its own proper functions, and cannot perform the part the hands and feet have had assigned to them.

Even so our Lord Jesus, the Son of Man, in whom the whole of human nature was gathered up and represented, had his own special work. He might have taught and done much that would have been of infinite value to us in our contact with the world. He confined himself to his calling, the making known, and the carrying out, the will of God in the saving of souls. Of all he was and did as Saviour, the cross is the sum and centre. And when he called some to come after him, and made the bearing of the cross the test of their fuller external discipleship, it was with the view of preparing and leaving behind him a body of men who, like himself, should learn to give their whole lives to the one work of carrying the cross, not simply as a means of personal sanctification, but as a continuance and living exhibition of his own crucifixion life, as the power that conquers the world. The more entirely these men gave themselves to this, their calling, the more they would be able to help those who had to act out the spirit of Christian discipleship in the midst of the vocations of this world. The separation of some to the more manifest crossbearing as abiding witnesses to its necessity and power, even though their help appears lost in the battle of daily life, would be the gain of all. The embodiment of the inmost spirit of the cross in the external life of some will avail much to remind those who have to live in exernal contact with the world what the spirit is they have to maintain.

Though the whole life of Christ was in the crucifixion spirit, yet the portion in which the cross was made manifest is that which brings us its greatest help. Even so, while the whole church has to bear the mark of the crucifixion spirit, it is those who have the burden or the privilege of specially manifesting it through whom the Lord will dispense his richest blessings.

It was the intensity of Paul's desire thus to know and represent and preach Christ as the crucified, that was the secret of counting all things loss, and his glorying in affliction as the means of fellowship with his cross. It was the consuming desire to be partaker with the Lord in his suffering that made so many of the martyrs in suffering and death more than conquerors. It was this that even in

the darkest ages made men and women give up all for the
imitation of Christ and the following of him in his of pov-
erty and his servant form. It is this the church of our day
still needs, in the ministry and out of it – those who in the
deepest humility give themselves entirely to a life of separation, even from what is lawful and good to others,
that, in the interest of the church at large, the spiritual
may take complete possession of them.

And what will be the marks of this desire for closer
conformity to our Lord? Some have said that bearing the
cross means bearing reproach or persecution for his
sake. It surely means a great deal more. It must be to the
disciple what it was to the Master. And to him it was
indeed much more. It meant the giving up of his will in
Gethsemane, of his body to suffering and pain, of his life
to death. The cross was his acceptance of that judgment.
The giving up everything that has any connection with
sin to the death: it was his dying to the world and all it
offered that he might enter the life of God. And to the
disciple bearing the cross it means nothing less. The
cross is the power that crucified, gives up to death, and
slays everything that is of sinful nature, to make way for
the life of God. The cross is death; cross-bearing is giving
oneself willingly and unceasingly unto the death of
Christ. And where this is truly done in the faith of Christ,
there cross-bearing becomes a glorying in the cross,
because the victory and the life it won is imparted in
unceasing power. But this is only one side; the cross not
only means death, the way to life, but death for others.
The element of love is inseparable from the very thought
of the cross of Christ. And no one can bear his cross in
the right spirit and follow Christ, without discovering
that the added injunction, let him deny himself, means
more than he thought. Let him deny himself as Christ
did, let personal sanctification be only a means to an end
– the bringing life and blessing to others. The Holy Spirit
says: 'Be imitators of God ... And walk in love, as Christ
also hath loved us, and hath given himself for us ... a sacrifice to God.' The sacrifice of the cross was to God for

men. In the love of men it had its motive as much as in the will of God. True cross-bearing will ever bring both the will and the power to give ourselves for men, to yield ourselves to God as whole burnt sacrifices for men around us. Intense love for souls, the sacrifice of all to God that he may use us, the loss of self in the desire for others, is the true crucifixion spirit. Through death to life, through a death to self to a life of love for others: this is cross-bearing.

This is the life to which Jesus called all his disciples in their measure, but which he specially enjoined upon his immediate followers. This is the life of which the church of the nineteenth century has special need. There are many souls who are free and do love to give themselves wholly to such a life. But they have heard so much of the sin of withdrawing themselves from ordinary society and vocations that they have been afraid. They thought if they did it, it would be like saying all ought to do it, or like professing to be better than others. Let them not be afraid. Let them boldly – he that is born of God, and like Christ – give themselves in love a sacrifice for men.

When once the Spirit has taken possession of us, or even when once we have yielded ourselves to it that it may take possession, what new meaning will be given for every call for self-denial, or the sacrifice of money or comfort for the sake of God's work. To Christ, the privilege of having a body, and a will, and a life, and a soul, and a spirit, was that he might sacrifice them to God for men. When this Christ-Spirit enters us, the question of how much we must give is changed into how much we may give, because giving becomes transfigured into a fellowship with Christ's giving himself. The glory of the cross shines through all our life, as it delivers from the world and self with all that pleases them, and gives everything we possess a new value with the one thought: I can sacrifice it for God and for men: I can give it to God to bless men.

Chapter 10

Deny Self and Take the Cross Daily

'If any man will come after me, let him deny himself, and take up his cross daily, and follow me. For whosoever will save his life shall lose it: but whosoever will lose his life for my sake, the same shall save it.' Luke 9:23–24

Follow me! How little the disciples knew what they were beginning when they obeyed that call. And yet they made no mistake in doing so, and never had reason to regret it because it was the call of Christ, the Son of God. All unwittingly they gave themselves into the charge of ominpotent love. In his keeping they were safe. When we begin to feel how little we have understood the meaning of the call, let this be our comfort. To follow Jesus, to think and act, to live and suffer like him – how impossible unless we have a heart, a nature, a life wholly like his. But it becomes possible when we begin to know that because he is divine, he has a power of working within us, of breathing into us the will and the power indeed to follow him, and to prove that we are of one Father with him, and of one Spirit too. Let us entrust ourselves to him with the confidence that he will lead us in his own steps and in his own strength. We shall need the lesson in the teaching our text of today has to bring.

In our previous meditation we saw how deep and intimate the relation between the disciple's taking his cross and his following Christ. Here we have an additional thought suggested. Let him deny himself, and take up his cross, and follow me: the deepest root of the cross-bearing and the following is here uncovered. Even while the Christian is striving earnestly to follow Christ, and in some measure to take his cross, there is a secret power that resists and opposes and prevents. The very man who is praying and vowing and struggling to follow fully what desire and will and heart are apparently set on, in his inmost self refuses the cross his Lord has called him to. Self, the real centre of his being, the controlling power, refuses to accept. And so Christ teaches Peter, and us, when he for the second time speaks of taking the cross, that it must commence with the total denial of self. The cross means death; taking the cross, means the acceptance of and surrender to death; self, the real inner life of the person, must die: the taking up the cross and the following of Jesus will be unceasing failure, unless the beginning is made here: let him deny himself and take up his cross. He that losseth his life shall find it.

And why is it that our Saviour speaks thus, and makes a demand so high, so apparently unnatural, so difficult of fulfilment? Has not the love of life been implanted by the Creator? And is it not a sacred charge from him that I keep it? And Christ calls me to hate, to lose my life, to deny that which gives life its value, that which I am in my own proper person – to deny myself. And why is this life to be put first under the cross, and then on the cross? And why, if he died for me on the cross, and won life for

me, why must I still die, deny myself and daily take up
my cross?

The answer is simple, and yet not easy to understand.
Only to the soul that consents to obey Jesus before it
understands will the real spiritual answer be opened up.
Through the sin of Adam the life of man fell out of its
high estate, where it was a vessel in which God made his
power and blessedness to work, and fell under the power
of this world, in which the god of this world has his rule
and his dominion. And so man has become a creature
possessed of a strange, unnatural, worldly life. The will
of God, and heaven, and holiness, for which he was
created, have become darkened and lost to him. The
pleasures of the flesh, and of the world, and of self,
which are all the dark accursed workings of the evil
spirit, have become natural and attractive. Man sees
not, knows not, how sinful, wretched and deadly they
are – alienated from God, and all bearing within them
the very seeds of hell. And this self, this inmost root of
man's life, which he loves so well, is just the concentration of all that is not of God, but of the evil one. With a
great deal of what is naturally beautiful and seemingly
good, the power of self and its pride corrupts all and
makes it the very seat of sin, and death, and hell.

Jesus said, 'He that followeth me shall not walk in
darkness, but shall have the light of life.' He that makes
perfect conformity to the life and spirit of Jesus his aim,
will have a divine enlightenment from the life within. In
that light he will learn to see the exceeding hatefulness of
self: how it was this that drove out and supplanted the
first life of God; how it was this that crucified the Lord
Jesus, and is the cause of all the sin and wretchedness in
the world. He will see how there is nothing so good and
right and blessed as to have this self conquered and cast
out to make way for the life in God and to God, which
Christ brings; and how all that man can do is simply to
deny self at every step and yield to Christ. And when
once one has consented to this life and of the entire
denial of self, the crown will be welcomed and loved as

the appointed power of God for freeing us of the evil power that is the only hindrance in our way of being fully conformed to the image of God's Son loving and serving the Father even as he did. To deny self is the inner spirit, of which taking the cross is the manifestation.

Let him deny himself, and take the cross daily, and follow me. The insight into what the denial of self means makes clear why the cross must be taken up daily. It is not only special trial or suffering that calls to it; in the time of quiet and prosperity the need is still more urgent. Self is the enemy that is ever near and ever seeking to regain its power. When he came down from the third heaven Paul was in danger of being exalted; the denial of self and the bearing of the cross is to be the everyday spirit. When Paul says, 'I have been crucified with Christ'; 'Far be it from me to glory except in the cross ... by which the world has been crucified to me, and I to the world;' he speaks of himself as living each moment the crucifixion life. It was not a thing to be remembered at times, to be put on on special occasions – his whole life, day by day, bore the mark of the cross. What Jesus spake before he had died on the cross, of the disciple taking his cross, was nothing else than the bud of which Paul's 'crucified with Christ' is the fruit. Taking the cross daily means to us, now that we know what Christ's cross has brought to us, nothing less than our daily renewed acceptance of our fellowship with our crucified Lord. Nothing less than this is the secret of life and holiness and power – abiding even in Christ the crucified one, glorying in the cross by which I have been and now am crucified.

You may have seen the device of a hand holding a cross, with the motto 'Teneo et Tenem' – 'I hold and am held', or, to put it more freely, 'I bear and am borne'. The words used before the cross of Christ were fully known – Take thy cross – express the former idea: Accept thy cross and bear it. The words given by the Holy Spirit after the crucified One had been glorified and revealed as our life – 'crucified with Christ' – point more to the other side: Believe that his cross, that he the crucified one, bears thee. Before the work was finished it was only – Take thy cross; now the finished work is revealed, that is, taken up and transfigured in the higher – crucified with Christ. I bear the cross and am borne. 'I have been crucified with Christ: Christ liveth in me.' It is only in the power of being borne that we can bear.

How wide is the application of the command: Deny self, and take the cross daily. And how impossible in our own strength the fulfilment. We are what Kempis says, 'To resist the appetites of the body and bring them in absolute subjection to the Spirit; to shun honours; to receive affronts with meekness; to be content to be despised by others, to bear with calm resignation the loss of fortune, health and friends; to have no desire after the riches, the honours, and the pleasures of the world: this is not the effect of any power which is inherent in man, but in the pure fruit of the grace of Christ, operating so powerfully in the fallen soul as to make it embrace that which it would naturally abhor and shun. If you depend upon your own will and strength to do and suffer all this, you will find yourself as unable to accomplish it as to create another world. But if you turn to the divine power within yourself, and trust only to that as the doer and sufferer of all, the strength of omnipotence will be imparted to you, and the world and the flesh shall be put under your feet.' This is the strength that comes to him who truly speaks in faith: 'I am crucified with Christ ... Christ liveth in me.' I can deny self, and take the cross daily, because I follow him.

Yes, what first was put as a condition we had to fulfil if we we were to follow him, becomes its blessed fruit. When we hear the call, 'Follow me', we think chiefly of all it implies in us. It is needful we do so. But it is not the chief thing. A trusted leader takes all the responsibility of the way, and makes every provision. As we think of denying self, and taking the cross daily, we feel how little we know what it all means, how little we are able to perform what we do know. We need to fix our heart upon

Jesus, who calls us to take the cross and follow him. On Calvary he led the way and opened it for us, even to the throne of God's power. Let us fix our heart upon him: As he led his disciples, he will lead us. The cross is a mystery. Taking the cross is a deep mystery. Crucified with Christ is the deepest mystery of redemption. The hidden wisdom of God is a mystery. Let us follow Christ with the true desire to come after him, and live wholly as he to the glory of the Father, and enter through death with him into fullness of life with him as our leader. He will teach us, he will give us, he will make us that we know not. Lord Jesus, in thy name and strength, under thy guidance, I will deny myself, take my cross daily, and follow thee.

Chapter 11

The Cross the Way to God

'Christ also died for sins once, the righteous for the unrighteous, that he might bring us to God.' 1 Peter 3:18

Christ came to open up the way, and bring us back to God. It was God who created us for himself: that he might be our blessedness and we his: that we might have our abode in him, and he in us. It is God we have lost through sin; it is to God Christ would win and take us back. God is more, infinitely more, than salvation, and than heaven: God is the eternal life and eternal love who longs to live in us, and to fill us with his love and with himself. For this Christ came; for this he suffered; that he might bring us to God.

The cross is the only way for human nature to come to God. It is the path in which Christ walked himself; the path which he opened for us; the path in which we too walk; the path in which alone we can lead others.

1. When our blessed Lord took our human nature with all its burden of sin and curse, he submitted to all the conditions of our human feebleness, and gave himself to be and to do all that a true man needed to be and do as God's creature. That he might show us what it means to be a creature, and how a creature should act; that he might make it possible for us to live as a creature should; he humbled himself to live the life of a creature. He not only grew and became strong; he not only advanced in stature but in wisdom too, and in favour with God and man. Through his whole life there was a true human development. In the gradual opening up to him of the will of God; in his learning obedience, and being made perfect through suffering; in his life of temptation and suffering; in his preparation for his final sacrifice; in all things he became like us. And so the cross was to him, as man and Mediator, the only path by which, in our nature, he could come to God.

The cross speaks of sin: it was only as admitting to the full and bearing the evil of sin, as hatred against God, that man could come to God. The cross speaks of curse; God's judgment against sin; as long as man did not accept and approve that judgment as righteous, there could be no thought of his being restored to God's presence. The cross speaks of suffering: it is only as, in suffering, the will of God is accepted and everything given up to it, that there could be union with God. The cross speaks of death: it is only as man is ready to part utterly and entirely with his whole present life, to die to it, that he can enter into, or fully receive into himself, the life and glory of God. All this Christ did. His whole life was animated by the crucifixion spirit. The cross on Calvary was simply fruit that had been growing and ripening all through his life. All along it had been a protest against man's sin; a witness to the righteousness of God's judgment against it: a readiness in everything to give up his will, and bear any suffering, that the Father's honour might be vindicated: a determination to sacrifice life itself as the only way by which our human nature could be fitted and transformed for the indwelling of God. The way of the cross was the way in which Jesus as man personally walked his whole life through, that as our forerunner, he might enter in and appear before God for us. 'Through thee things which he suffered: and being made perfect, he became the author of eternal salvation unto all them that obey him.' For Jesus himself the cross was the path to God.

2. All that our Lord was and did and did as man had an infinite worth. He was not only man but God. As the Son of God and heir of all things the world and man had been created by him, and in him, and for him. In virtue of his divine nature, possessing and filling all things. He became the second Adam, a new head here upon earth for the human race. As such, his bearing the cross, and entering into God's holy presence, was the opening up of a way in which we too could draw nigh. His death, the bearing of God's judgment on sin, was the putting away of sin; he made an end of sin. In bearing the condemnation and the curse and death, he bore away the sin; he abolished, broke the power of him that had the power of death, and set us his prisoners free. The cross, and the blood, and the death of Christ are God's assurance to the sinner that there is an immediate acquittal to each one who will accept of and entrust himself to this Saviour, and an everlasting admission to God's favour and friendship. All the claims that God's law had against us: all the power sin and Satan had over us; all are at an end: the death of Jesus was the death of sin and death. The path of the cross is the path Christ has opened for us; in it we have full liberty and power to draw near to God.

3. In that path of the cross we now have to walk if we are to come to God.

The entrance to that path is repentance and faith. As men listen to the charge God's messenger has against them: 'This Jesus ye crucified', and yield to it: as with penitent hearts they ask how they are to be delivered, the Gospel tells them that the cross that reveals the sin has taken it away, and that the Christ against whom they have sinned has in his love won for them pardon and life. The man who learns to know his sin at the cross, learns to know his Saviour there too. Faith in the cross, and its perfect redemption, sets a man at once in the way of life. The path of the cross is the path that brings us to God.

Continuance in that path is no less by faith. But a faith that sees more of the spiritual meaning of the cross, longs for a fuller experience of its redeeming power in victory over sin, yields more completely to its fellowship and dominion, trusts with larger confidence in the completeness of its deliverance from the world and the flesh. This faith sees how the crucified Christ is indeed the revelation of all that is holy and lovely before God, and how there is no beauty or blessedness in heaven greater than to have his disposition, to bear the cross after him and like him, and to allow his Spirit from heaven to act in us as in him, as the Spirit of the cross. Above all, this faith learns how the death of Christ is a finished and everlasting redemption, not only as an atonement made once for all, but equally as a death once for all to sin, and a life unto God, to be imparted and is wrought in all who desire and believe it. If there were no path for Christ to God but through death, the entire giving up of life, how much more this must be the only path in which the sinner can come to be filled with the life of God. And now that Christ's death is a finished thing, the death and the life we receive in him is the power of such absolute surrender working in us, with the blessed indwelling in which it leads. It is this faith that enables a man to say joyfully: 'I am crucified with Christ.' 'I glory in the cross, by which I am crucified to the world.' The crucifixion spirit, with its protest against and separation from the world, its sacrifice of all self-pleasing. and its absolute surrender to God even to death, marks the whole life and walk. The cross daily borne and glorified in becomes indeed the path to God.

4. In this path we can win and bless others. It was as

the crucified, giving his life for man, that Christ won the power to bless them. It was his full acceptance of the sufferings of Christ on the way to glory of which Peter speaks in his first epistle, which filled him with boldness to testify for the Lord. It was the intensity of Paul's desire for perfect conformity to his Lord's sufferings that gave him his power as an apostle. In the measure in which the church gives itself to God, a sacrifice for men, will the power of God's Spirit work through her. It is Christ crucified who saves men: it is Christ crucified living and breathing in us who can, who will use us for his saving work. And his living and working in us means nothing less than that we, like him, are ready to give our lives for others. That means – to forget ourselves, to sacrifice ourselves, to suffer anything that the lost may be won.

At first when a soul enters into the truth of being crucified with Christ, and bearing about his dying in the body, the chief thought is that of personal sanctification. Death to sin, death to the world, death to self are regarded as the path of life and blessing to the soul. But these desires cannot lead it in truth to trust in Christ as him in whom alone the death and the life out of death is known and found, without the contact with him opening up the secret that all his obedience to the Father and victory over sin was not for any personal glorification but for the saving of others around him. And the believer learns that the path of the cross cannot be trod truly by any who are not willing to work and give their life for others. And that, on the other hand, the only true power to bless others comes when the cross, as death to the world and self, becomes the law of our daily life. Christ walked in the path of the cross, and there won the power to open it to us. We walk in it, in our union to him, as we look upon our life as something to be entirely given away to our fellowmen, that the life of God may do its work through us. The cross was Christ's way to God – for himself and for us: for himself that it might be for us. The cross is our way to God – for ourselves and for others: for ourselves that it may be so for others too.

The church is continually speaking of the secret of power in its ministry of salvation. How little it is understood that its only power over the world is, to be crucified to the world. It is Christ crucified, a stumbling-block and foolishness to men, gloried in by those who can say, 'I am crucified with Christ,' it is the preaching of the cross thus known and gloried in that is the power of God.

Chapter 12

The Triumph of the Cross

*'Blotting out the handwriting of ordinances
that was against us, which was contrary to us,
and took it out of the way, nailing it to his
cross; And having spoiled principalities and
powers, he made a show of them openly,
triumphing over them in it.'*
Colossians 2:14–15

*'Now thanks be unto God, which always
causeth us to triumph in Christ, and maketh
manifest the saviour of his knowledge by us of
every place.'* 2 Corinthians 2:14

When God placed Adam in paradise it is evident that
there must have been some power of evil against which
he had to watch and guard it. As all that God created

during the six days were very good, the evil must have been in existence previously. Scripture does not reveal how and whence it came: it is enough that it exists and threatens the very centre of the new creation, the garden of God and the dwelling of man, with danger and ruin. God seeks to rob this evil of its power, and purposes doing so through the medium of man. The thought naturally suggests itself whether man may not have been created for this very purpose, to conquer the evil that had existed before him. It is this that constitutes this apparently insignificant earth the historic centre of the universe, that just here where the power through whom most probably chaos had been caused (Gen 1:2), in the very world raised out of the ruins of its previous kingdom, still sought to maintain its hold – that just here man was created to conquer and cast it out. It is this that makes this world of such importance in the eyes of God and his angels; it is the battle-field where heaven and hell meet in deadly conflict.

When man listened to the word of the serpent instead of the word of God, and took it up into his heart and life, he came under the power and rule of the god of this world. That word of the serpent was but as a seed. The terrible history of mankind can never be rightly understood till we allow Scripture to teach us that, even as there is a purpose in God which overrules all, so there is, on the other hand, amid what appears nothing but a natural growth and development, an organised system and kingdom that holds rule over man, that keeps them in darkness, and uses them in its war against the kingdom of God's Son. On a scale of which we can form little conception, through the slow length of ages which God's patience bears, amid all the liberty of human will and action, there is an unceasing contest going on. Though the issue is not doubtful, the struggle is long and destructive. In the history of that struggle the cross is the turning point.

When Christ came to save men, before he entered his public ministry, he had first to meet God. In his baptism

he entered into fellowship with sinners, and gave himself
to fulfil all righteousness; in the vision of the opened
heaven and the descending dove, as in the voice of the
Father, he received the seal of divine approval. He then
had to meet the tempter, through whom Adam had fallen; only then could he begin his ministry among men.
As definitely as Christ in the work of salvation had to
deal with God and with man had he to deal with Satan
too. There was no salvation possible, but as Satan's
power was acknowledged, and met, and overthrown.

It was even so at the close of his life in his great
redeeming work. If we want to understand this we must
not only think of the part God and man had in his sufferings, and in which relation his redemption stood to
them, but also what the place which Satan, as the prince
of this world, held. Listen to what he spoke of his passion: 'Now is the judgment of this world: now shall the
prince of this world be cast out.' 'The prince of this world
cometh, and hath nothing in me.' 'This is your hour, and
the power of darkness.' The words lift the veil and show
us the dark background whence the suffering and the
struggle of Christ had its reality and its terror. As long as
we refuse to give it its full weight, we shall never understand either the nature of Christ and our relation to the
world, nor what it cost him, nor what a redemption has
been actually accomplished, nor what now is the battle
we as the redeemed of the Lord have to wage against the
powers of darkness and the world in which they rule.

In our text we have a wonderful lifting of the veil to
show in what the redemption of the cross implies. Having put off from himself the principalities and the powers, he made a show of them openly, triumphing over
them in it (i.e. in his cross). In the darkness of the cross
the powers of darkness had made their onslaught:
together they pressed on him with everything that is terrible in their power, surrounding him with the very darkness and misery of hell. They formed a cloud so thick and
dark that the very light of God's face forsook him. But
he put them off from himself; he beat back the enemies

and overcame the temptation. He made a show of them openly: in all the spirit world, before angels and devils, it was known that he conquered. The very grave gave up its dead. And so he triumphed over them. He led them in triumph as prisoners: their power for ever broken, the gate of the prison-house in which they hold men captive broken open, and liberty proclaimed to all their prisoners. The prince of this world is now cast out. He no longer has power to hold in bondage those who long for deliverance. He now only rules over those who consent to be his slaves. There is now a perfect deliverance for all who yield themselves to Christ and his cross.

The cross is a triumph: this is the great lesson of our text. The cross is a triumph, which began when Christ cried: It is finished. It is the beginning of a triumphal procession in which Christ moves on through the world in hidden glory, leading captivity captive, leading into liberty his ransomed ones. And the believer can now rejoice. 'Thanks be unto God, which always causeth us to triumph in Christ.' Every thought of the cross, every step under the cross, every proclamation of the cross, ought to be in the tone of a divine triumph. 'Death is swallowed up in victory ... But thanks be to God, who gives us the victory through our Lord Jesus Christ.'

Without this our apprehension of the meaning and our experience of the power of the cross, must be defective. We shall find this both in our personal life and in our labours for others. In our personal life the cross will be counted a burden: the call to bear it, a law hard to obey: the attempt to live the crucifixion life, a failure; the thought of a daily death, a weariness. To crucify the flesh demands such unceasing watchfulness and self-denial that it is given up as a hopeless or fruitless task. It cannot be otherwise, until we know in some measure that the cross is a triumph. We have not to crucify the flesh: it has been done in Christ. The act of crucifixion on Calvary is a finished transaction: the life and spirit that goes forth from it works in unceasing power. The call to us is to believe, to be of good cheer. Nothing less than his death can suffice us: nothing less than his death is at our disposal. 'Thanks be unto God, which always causeth us to triumph in Christ.'

Of no less consequence is it, in our service in the world, that we believe in the triumph of the cross over the powers of darkness. Nothing less than an insight into this truth can teach us to know the supernatural strength and the spiritual subtlety of our enemy. Nothing less can teach us what must be our object as we wrestle 'against the rulers of the darkness of this world' – the bringing men away out from the world and the power of its prince. Nothing less than this, an insight into the triumph the cross has won and ever given, can make us take our true position, as the instruments and servants of our conquering king, whose one hope is to be led in triumph in him. And nothing less can keep alive in us the courage and the hope which we need in our impotence as the mighty power of the enemy ever force themselves on us. Faith must learn to say in all its service and warfare, 'Thanks be unto God, which always causeth us to triumph in Christ.' The cross with its foolishness and weakness, its humiliation and shame, is the everlasting signal of the victory Christ hath won by weapons not of this warfare, of the victory the church and every servant of Christ can continually win as he enters more deeply into the spirit of his crucified Lord, and so yields more fully to him.

Most of us know the story of Constantine's vision of the cross. On the eve of a battle with an enemy stronger than himself, he called upon the Christian God to help him. Soon after, so Eusebius relates, there was seen in the heavens in a stream of light the form of a cross with the inscription over it: 'In hoc signo vinces.' 'In this sign thou shalt conquer.' As he thought over the vision, Christ appeared to him in a dream, holding a cross, and commanded him to place it on his banner. It filled his soldiers with courage, and led them to victory.

Whatever we may think of the story, it is an exquisite symbol of the very truth the church needs in these days.

In this sign you shall conquer. If you want to have the victory over self and sin, over the flesh and the world – in this sign you shall conquer. Ask your Lord to give you in his light a vision of the cross in the heavens over you. Ask him to set upon you and all around you the sign of the cross, with its curse and its blessing, its death and its life, its weakness and its strength, its shame and its glory. He speaks: Fear not, be of good cheer; I have overcome the world. In this sign you shall conquer.

As we look out upon the world, and see its terrible power without and within the church, and think of the powers of darkness with which we have to contend, let us look up and gaze upon the heavenly vision. In this sign you shall conquer. Let God's childen but determine not to know in heart, or life, or love, anything save Jesus Christ and him crucified: let them give themselves up to let him who died upon the cross live in them and work in them his separation from the world, for the world and victory will surely come. Under the banner of the cross victory is sure. 'Thanks be unto God, which always causeth us to triumph in Christ.' And may the vision never fade from our heart.

Chapter 13

The Death of the Cross

'Obedient unto death, even the death of the cross.' Philippians 2:8

Death is the central thought of the cross. In choosing it, on man's part as on God's, death was its one aim. It is death that gave it its terror; it is death that now gives it its attraction, and power to bless.

What means this solemn, awful cross? A death. An accursed death. A violent death; the work of man's rejection of God's Son; the proof of man's enmity against God. A judicial death. God's condemnation of sin in his own Son, 'made sin', 'made a curse for us.' A sacrificial death: the blessed Son yielding himself an offering for sin. A death of suffering and agony, even to the being forsaken of God in thick darkness. A death through sin, and for sin, and so the death of sin. A death in which the love of God revealed its measureless riches; in which the love of the Son laid hold upon us, and delivered us from the power of the enemy. A death that was the death of death swallowed up in victory. A death that became the path of life to the Lord of glory, the one cause of his exaltation to the throne of God as our mediator, that is now to us also the gate of life. A death that is the source of life to all the redeemed, its experience and fellowship and conformity the object of their highest desires. A death which in the glory of heaven is ever celebrated in songs of praise and gladness.

The death of the cross, it is indeed 'the mystery of God', 'the hidden wisdom of God in a mystery.' Would God that the Holy Spirit might reveal its power in our heart. Blessed Spirit, give thou us the interpretation of the wonderful sign of the cross, work thou in us the full participation of its death and the redemption it wrought.

1. Look at the death of the cross, and man's part in it, and see it as the fruit of sin. And that in more than one sense. Sin brings forth death; it can end in nothing else. The sinner can do nothing but destroy. From Abel at the gate of paradise to Christ on Calvary, we have the proof that where sin reigns, it works death. Satan is a murderer from the beginning. Self under the power of sin will, when irritated and let loose, stop short of nothing less than the death of all who oppose it. Sin can only destroy. And so when the Son of God came, and waged war against sin, it rose up and slew him. And the cross with its death stands there to tell us that it is the very nature of sin and sinful man to slay and destroy.

And so it destroys, too, the sinner himself. All sin is suicide. The very essence of sin is death: without sin death is an impossibility; with sin death is an absolute eternal necessity. Sin is separation from God, the only fountain of life. Man can have no life but in God. Sin is simply the loss of God and the loss of the life that is in him. When our blessed Lord became man, he was the sinless, holy one, and there could be no thought of death being a necessity with him. But because, as the holy one, he united himself to our race, as the seed of David and of Adam, became one with us, he came under the awful possibility of death. As the holy One, he might, if the Father had withdrawn the commandment to lay down his life, have ascended to heaven from the Mount of Transfiguration. But he would have gone alone. As Mediator, he had identified himself with us in a way that passes understanding; he had taken hold of us and embraced us, so that 'he was made sin' – and bore our sin. And his death on the cross was the awful proof of the terrible and destructive nature of sin. When the very Son of God joined himself to us, sin slew him. Though himself divinely and absolutely free from sin, he could not touch the sinner without drawing the death-poison into himself. He became obedient to the death of the cross that we might learn what an accursed thing sin is – nothing but death and destruction. If men would only learn it, and hate and flee the serpent's power.

2. Look at the death of the cross, and God's part in it, and see in it the judgment of God. Sin is not only the loss of life, as a thing we possess, but of the living God in whom is the life. We not only sin against ourselves, but against a God, who feels the sin, is grieved by it, and must judge and condemn it. The death of the cross not only reveals the nature of sin, but that righteousness of God in which the death that sin works has its power. 'The strength of sin is the law.' This is the fearfulness and abomination of sin, that it can reach God, and wound his very heart. This is its accursedness, that it rouses God's indignation, and exposes his creature to his everlasting condemnation. And this is the mystery and the glory and the power of the cross, that in the crucified Christ God condemned sin in the flesh. 'He bore our sins in his body on the tree.' They were on him, with all the sufferings, and curse, and condemnation, and death-agony which being forsaken of God implies – for that is what sin necessitates, and what Christ bore.

This was all God's work. As truly as the cross reveals man's heart, does it reveal the heart of God. His righteousness which never can tolerate sin. His love to the sinner which gave the Son. His righteousness which provided and accepted the sacrifice. His love which now receives the sinner to his side. The death of the cross is to the Father the perfect obedience of his Son and the full surrender into his hands – a sweet-smelling savour:

3. Look at the death of the cross, and Christ's part in it, and see there the path he opened through death to life. We must not only look at the atonement as the fruit of the cross, but deeper down at that which gave the atonement its value: Christ's absolute surrender of himself into the Father's hands in death. This was the life the creature was to have lived: even giving up his life and will to God, for God's life and will to fill it. This was what sin had refused: man would have a life and will of his own. This was what Christ came to restore. He gave himself to endure what it was agony and blood-sweat even to think of; he allowed his life to be taken away; he gave up his holy life to the power and suffering of death. He entered the darkness of death and the grave in the trust that the Father would give him a new life in his glory. He parted with the life he had in his connection with us in our sin, in the assurance that he would win for himself and us the fullness of the life of heaven. And so he taught us the great lesson, that death is the path to life; that to give up all for and to God is the way to get all from God; that there is no way to God and perfect fellowship and likeness but through the giving up of all one has, of one's very spirit, into the Father's hands. And so he opened for us the new and living way into the holiest of all through death – his death for us, and our death with him.

4. Look now, once more, at the death of the cross, and our part in it as believers. The way through death to life which Jesus opened up for himself as our forerunner, he opened for us too. The cross comes to us with the message that there is no way of getting rid of the sinful life but by dying to it; that there is no way of dying to it but by first acknowledging the curse that is on it and death as its due reward, and then accepting him who has died the

death for us and makes us partakers of it. He that believes in Christ the crucified, and receives him into his heart, is baptised unto his death by a spirit baptism. That death of the cross with all its dispositions and power and working is ours; we have been crucified with Christ, are dead indeed unto sin and alive unto God. The death and the life are in us as in Christ the two forces that work out the glory: as we daily enter deeper into the death, we ever rise stronger in the life. And as our eyes are opened to what the death means and brings we begin with Paul to count all things loss to know Christ – how passing strange – in the fellowship of his sufferings, being made conformable to his death. The proverb of the early ages, 'Death, the Gate of Life', becomes the key to all the secrets of the life of sanctification and of service.

In striving to learn and hold this blessed truth, many a mistake may still be made. How often a man may strive to die, or think he must crucify himself and put the old life to death. How often he may be looking within to see or feel whether he be dead, and mourn: not yet utterly dead to sin. He will have to learn how this death and the life in it and out of it is all in Christ and by faith. He will have to come back to the world and say – apart from what he sees or feels – I am indeed utterly dead to sin. God says it because it is so: in Christ, as Christ, I am indeed dead to sin, for the life in me, and the living I in me, is the life out of death that is in Christ in heaven. He will find that just as simply as it was at his first conversion – Jesus only, so it is in the appropriation of the fuller blessing of the fellowship of the cross. St Paul says: 'I am crucified with Christ … yet not I, but Christ liveth in me … I live by faith of the Son of God, who loved me.' It is Christ himself who breathes and lives his own crucifixion spirit in us: it is Christ alone who gives his mind within us, and makes his humility and the obedience unto death our own.

The death of the cross – through eternity this was the deepest thought of God's heart. Through his whole life this was the one purpose of Christ's heart. Through all the heavens there is no symbol of love and power and glory like this. I will ask my God to plant his cross in my heart. I will ask my Lord, at his highest grace, to reveal his death in me. Through all the riches of his glory there is no higher blessing than this: the death of the cross.

Chapter 14

The Crucifixion of the World

'God forbid that I should glory, save in the cross of our Lord Jesus Christ, by whom the world is crucified unto me, and I unto the world.' Galatians 6:14

We have come to one of the most important chapters of our book. There is not a question of greater interest in the church of our day than that which deals with her relation to the world. And perhaps not one of greater difficulty. The world itself is of such large and varied meaning, that it is not easy to define. The spirit of the world is so subtle and universal; we have been so born and bred under its influence; the power of the god of this world, blinding the eyes, is still so strong in all believers who do not very specially seek enlightened eyes of the heart through the Holy Spirit: our whole natural life is in such close contact with it, that it needs very special grace to know fully what the world as revealed by the cross really is, and what the position in it to which the cross commits us. Our only hope is in the teaching of him who gave himself to draw us out of this present evil world.

The meaning of the word as Christ used, is simple. He used the expression of mankind in its fallen state, and its alienation from God. He regarded it as an organised system or kingdom, the very opposite and the mortal enemy of his kingdom, with a mighty unseen power, the god of this world, ruling it, and a spirit, the spirit of this world, pervading it and giving it strength. He more than once gave this as his special characteristic, 'I am not of the world.' He also taught his disciples, 'ye are not of the world.' He warned them that because they were not of the world, the world would hate them as it had hated him. Of his sufferings he spake: 'The prince of this world cometh and findeth nothing in me.' 'This is your hour and the power of darkness.' 'Be of good cheer, I have overcome the world.' In the hatred that nailed him to the cross the world revealed its true spirit, under the power of its god. In the cross Christ revealed his spirit, his rejection of the world with all its threats and promises. The cross is the seal of his word, that his kingdom is not of this world. The more we love the cross and live by it, the more we shall know what the world is, and be separate from it.

In the beloved disciple the contrast comes out as strongly. 'If any man love the world, the love of the Father is not in him.' 'The world knoweth us not, because it knew him not.' 'They are of the world, therefore speak they of the world, and the world heareth them. We are of God, he that knoweth God heareth us.' 'Whatsoever is begotten of God overcometh the world.' 'We know that we are of God, and the whole world lieth in wickedness.' The difference and antagonism between the two kingdoms is irreconcilable. However much the world be externally changed by Christian influence, its nature remains the same. However close and apparently

favourable the alliance between the world and the
church, the peace is but hollow and for a time. When the
cross is fully preached with its revelation of sin and
curse, with its claim to be accepted and borne – the
enmity is speedily seen. And nothing can overcome the
world but that which is begotten of God.

In our text we see how clearly Paul felt, and how
boldly he proclaimed, the enmity between the cross and
the world, 'I glory in the cross, through which the world
hath been crucified to me, and I to the world.' He was so
identified with the cross that its relation to the world was
his. The cross was the separation between them. The
cross was the sign of the world's condemnation of Christ:
Paul accepted it; he was crucified by the world and to it.
The cross was God's condemnation of the world: Paul
saw the world condemned and under the curse. The
cross was the everlasting separation between himself
and the world as it is. The cross alone could be their
meeting place and reconciliation. It was for this he
gloried in the cross and preached it as the only power to
draw men out of the world to God.

The view many Christians take is the opposite of that
of Christ and John and Paul. They speak as if in some
way the curse had been taken off the world, and its
nature somehow softened. They think of educating and
winning the world, by meeting it more than half-way,
with offers of friendship. They regard the work of the
church as being to permeate the world with a Christian
spirit and take possession of it. They do not see that the
spirit of the world permeates the church and takes possession of it to a far larger extent. The offence of the
cross is done away with, and the cross is so adorned with
the flowers of earth that the world is quite content to give
it a place among the idols. No wonder we complain of
the lack of conversions. Nothing can convert men but
the gospel of the cross: that, in its foolishness, is the
power of God to salvation. The cross in its naked
simplicity, with its judgment of the world and all that is
in the world, with its discovery of the spirit of the world

as enmity against God, and there, with its infinite love
and its finished redemption, offered to each one who will
forsake the world and take up the cross – this cross alone
is the wisdom and power of God.

In war there is no greater danger than underrating the
power of the enemy. The work of the church is a war, an
unceasing battle. 'We wrestle not against flesh and
blood, but against principalities, against powers, against
the rulers of the darkness of this world, against spiritual
wickedness in high places.' The world is sinful humanity,
not a mere collection of individual men, led on by blind
chance in their sin. It is an organised force, animated
unconsciously by one inspiring force, a power of darkness, led on by one leader, the god of this world.
'Wherein in time past ye walked according to the curse
of this world, according to the prince of the power of the
air, the spirit that now worketh in the children of dis-
obedience.' It is only as this truth is accepted in all its
bearings by the church, that it becomes capable of
understanding the meaning of the cross, that it can see
how it was meant to draw men out of the world, and that
it will have the courage to believe that nothing but the
persistent preaching of the cross in all its divine incom-
prehensibility, is what can overcome the world and save
men out of it. The powers of the other world, 'the
spiritual wickedness in high places,' working here in
men, can only be conquered and brought into subjection
by a higher power, the power of God, by him who 'having spoiled principalities and powers, he made a shew of
them openly, triumphing over them in it.' It is the cross,
the cross with its sin, and curse, and death, with its love
and life and triumph, which alone is the power of God.

The great power of the world consists in its darkness.
'The god of this world hath blinded the minds of the
unbelieving.' 'We wrestle against the rulers of the darkness of this world.' If any of the spirit of this world be
found in the believer or the church, just so far are they
incapable of seeing things in the light of God. They
judge spiritual truth with a heart that is prejudiced by the

spirit of the world in them. From this no honesty of purpose, no earnestness of thought, no power of intellect
can free them. They can understand and receive God's
truth no more than the very spirit of Christ and his cross
have expelled, or is truly sought after to expel, the spirit
of the world. The Holy Spirit, tenderly waited on and
yielded to, is the only light that can open the eyes of the
heart to see and know what is of the world and what is of
God. And the Holy Spirit is only truly yielded to, as the
cross, with its crucifixion of the flesh and the world, has
become the law of our life. The cross and the world are
diametrically and unchangeably opposed to each other.

This is the ruin that sin wrought. Man was to have
lived on earth in the power of the heavenly life, in fellowship with God and obedience to his will. When he sinned, he fell entirely under the power of this present visible world, as the god of this world rules it, and uses it as
a means of temptation and sin. His eyes closed to
spiritual and eternal things; those of time and sense mastered and ruled him. Some speak as if the cross of Christ
had so taken away the curse and power of sin in the
world that the believer is now free to enter into the
enjoyment of it without danger, that the church has now
the power of appropriating it, the calling to take possession of it for God. This is certainly not what Scripture
teaches. The cross moves the curse from the believer,
not from the world. Whatever has sin in it, has the curse
on it as much as ever. What the believer is to possess of
the world and its goods must first be sanctified by the
word and by prayer. Nothing but the discovery of the
evil of, and the deliverance from, the spirit of the world
by the cross and spirit of Christ, nothing but the spirit
and power of the cross animating us, separating and
freeing us from the spirit of the world, can keep us so
that we be in the world, but not of it. It cost Christ his
agony and bloodsweat, his awful death struggle, the sacrifice of his life, to conquer the world by the cross; nothing less than a full and hearty entrance into fellowship
with him into his crucifixion, can save us from its power.

In the epistle to the Galatians there are several passages having reference to the cross of Christ. Only one of them speaks definitely of the atonement, 'Christ hath redeemed us from the curse, being made a curse for us.' The others all bear upon the fellowship with the cross, and its relation to our inner life. When Paul says: 'I have been crucified with Christ, and I live no longer, but Christ liveth in me'; 'They that are Christ's have crucified the flesh'; 'I am crucified unto the world'; he speaks of a life, an inward disposition, a spiritual experience, in which the very spirit and power that animated Christ, when he bore the cross, is maintained and manifested. There are many who profess to make their boast in the cross, and count their faith in the righteousness of Christ as our justification before God, as the great proof of faithfulness to Scripture, and who yet, in their wholehearted enjoyment and toleration and participation of what is of the spirit of this world, prove that the glorying in a cross which crucifies the world has no real place in their religion. The cross that atones, and the world that crucified, are at peace. The cross that crucifies the world as an accursed thing, and keeps us crucified to it, is unknown.

If the preaching of the cross not only for justification but for sanctification, not only for pardon of sin but for power over the world, and an entire freedom from its spirit, is to take place in the church it had with Paul, we must beseech God to reveal what he means by the world, what he intends by the power of the cross. It is in the lives of men actually and manifestly crucified by the world and all that is of it, that the cross will prove its power.

Chapter 15

The Cross and its Intercession

'And when they were come to the place, which is called Calvary, there they crucified him ... Then said Jesus, Father, forgive them; for they know not what they do.' Luke 23:33–34

The 53rd chapter of Isaiah, in which the sufferings and death, the atonement and salvation of Christ are foretold, closes with these words: 'He bare the sin of many, and made intercession for the transgressors.' The great fruit and crown of his atoning work was to be the power of intercession, the right to ask and receive all he desired for those for whom he had died. The cross was needed to give efficacy to the intercession. If he had not given himself for men, he could not have interceded. Intercession was needed for the cross to prove its efficacy. Without intercession its blessings could not be claimed from God, or communicated to men. The cross and intercession are inseparable.

Intercession is born of the cross. When Christ was crucified his first words were a prayer for his murderers. Before this we never read of his praying for the unsaved. The prayer was the spontaneous expression of the spirit of the cross, the fit beginning of the seven words. It reveals the very heart of the crucified one – a love that embraces those who reject him, a love that forgets itself to present them to the Father as the one only desire of his heart. The love that gives itself to die is the love that must and will and can truly pray.

As closely linked as the cross and the intercession were upon earth, they are in heaven too. It was on the cross he won the right of intercession on the throne. Because he had proved his devotion to God and man on the cross, he was counted worthy that the power of asking, what he would should be given him. There is not a prayer he offers on the throne through the ages, but it owes its power to his death on the cross. His atonement for sin, his zeal for the honour of God, his self-sacrifice for men, were the proof that he had in very deed the heart of a true intercessor. And so intercession becomes the natural and inseparable fruit of the cross, the unceasing presentation to the Father of the atonement there accomplished, the unceasing obtaining from him and communicating to men of the blessings it has won.

In this work of intercession we, as the members of Christ's body, have an equal share with the head. Our faith in his cross is defective and terribly limited if it does not lead us to intercession. And, on the other hand, our intercession will be sadly lacking in power, unless it has its roots fixed deeply in the redemption of the cross. As the faith in its finished redemption, as the fellowship in its self-sacrifice and love, as the desire for its universal triumph animates us, our intercession will be in power. Let us study these three aspects of the truth, that, under the shadow of the cross, the life we owe to it may all be intercession.

1. The cross makes us intercessors by the faith it wakens in a finished redemption. And that both in regard to ourselves who pray, and to those for whom we pray.

As to ourselves, the great secret of boldness in interceding for others is the consciousness of influence with him to whom the request is made. When I can say: I am his intimate friend, he never refuses me, I am sure he will listen to my request; the work of intercession is easy. Even so with God: it is as we realise how infinitely pleasing we are to him, how delighted he is to see us come and boldly ask what we desire, that we shall draw near with liberty and confidence to plead for others. The cross gives us this assurance of being infinitely acceptable. As our faith sees how complete its work is, how every vestige of what could separate us from God is removed, and how the blood brings us so near, so very near to God, that we are as near as the Son himself, we hide ourselves in him, and boldly ask that he may be heard in us, and we be heard even as he is. There is no place for learning what it means, what a reality it is, to appear before God in Christ, as in intercesssion, when the measure of our boldness proves how fully we believe in the power of the cross.

This faith in the cross is equally our power of intercession when we think of those for whom we pray. The cross wakens hope for the darkest, most hardened and most hopeless of sinners. It tells us of a propitiation not for our sins only, but for the sins of the whole world. It is God's great seal to the declaration of his word concerning, 'God our saviour; who will have all men to be saved, who is longsuffering ... not willing that any should perish, but that all should come to repentance.' As we enter spiritually and practically into this will of God, as the actual and infinite desire of his love for the salvation of men, the strength of which is only to be measured by the sacrifice of the cross, we shall have the confidence of knowing that what we ask when we intercede for men, is according to his will, and will be given us. The cross, in the great world-wide efficacy of its redemption, will give us boldness and assurance in each individual case for which we plead its power.

2. The cross makes us intercessors by breathing into us its own spirit of self-sacrifice and love unto the death. In the beginning of the Christian life, the view we have been speaking of appears all we need – the cross and the work done on it, the all-prevailing plea for ourselves and those we pray for. But when we learn to ask why our prayers are not answered, why we have not come closer to God, the Holy Spirit shows us that our faith in the cross has been too much that of the intellect, and that its spirit has not yet fully possessed us. Nothing can have access to God, or be well pleasing to him, but what is like-minded to Christ. Our 'drawing nigh to God' in Christ does not only mean our union to him through a firm conviction that we are in him; that is only the beginning: abiding in Christ in order to pray in power means a life union in which his very life and spirit and disposition are the element in which we live. And because the cross was the crowning act for which the whole life of Christ on earth was lived, and the inspiration of all he did, as well as the seed out of which his life in glory was born, the cross is the simplest expression of what made him so pleasing to the Father. Therefore it is only as the spirit of the cross lives and reigns in us that we can receive power to use it and its finished work as our all-prevailing plea.

The cross is the highest revelation of the divine life as it has entered humanity to lead us back to the life we had lost. Its supreme lesson is: to die to the natural life, which is under sin, is the only way to live to God. The willingness to do so at any cost, the readiness to sacrifice everything to self to bring back God to men and men to God, the humility and love and self-devotion and utter surrender to and dependence on God, that characterised Jesus on his way to the cross, are what fitted him to be intercessor in heaven. We can take our share in his work of intercession only as the same spirit animates us. The

fellowship of the cross, cultivated in daily life, working
in humility and self-abnegation, revealing itself in absolute devotion to God and his righteousness, with
unbounded trust in his love to man, breathing itself out
in a love that has given itself to work and suffer, to live
and die for men – this it is that makes the intercessor. He
that aims at this with his whole heart, will find the power
of intercession grow into his life.

3. The cross makes us intercessors by pointing us to
the world it was meant to save. When men first receive
the cross as their life, it is mostly with the one thought of
personal salvation. Alas for those who rest content with
this: unwittingly they rob themselves of the true and full
blessing the cross can give. The cross is meant for the
world: he that would fully know its power and blessedness must take the world into his heart too. The cross in
the heart of God meant love to the world: in the heart of
God's child it must mean the same. In the heart of Christ
it meant nothing less: on the cross he at once began his
work of intercession for those nearest him. And his disciples learn from him, that whether at Jerusalem or in
the uttermost parts of the earth, every soul to whom the
cross has been given as the pledge of God's love, is to be
the object of our love, our labour, our intercession.

It is a strange but most blessed mystery that after God
had given his Son on the cross to work out the great
redemption, and placed him on the throne to dispense it
through the medium of his never-ceasing intercession,
he should need us to 'come to his help against the
mighty' powers of this world. Yet so it is. God seeks for
intercessors who really honour the cross by believing in
the power it has given them to prevail with him; who
really have received its spirit, its death and its life, into
their hearts, and live as crucified with Christ; and who
will now hold up the cross before him as their plea for his
blessing on those whom they want blessed. Adorable
mystery, that to us is committed this wonderful
stewardship of dispensing the salvation of the cross to
those for whom we intercede. Does not this give new

force to the words 'I have been crucified with Christ'? At first we only saw in it our justification. Then we thought it a great advance to see in it our sanctification, Christ's crucifixion life working in us. But now, must it not mean that one who has been crucified with Christ not only takes his place as a justified man, not only receives his Spirit to make him a sanctified man but becomes a partner in his work and the power for that work. Crucified with Christ can mean nothing less than this: set free from the natural life of self, a sacrifice and an offering to God for the salvation of men. This was what it meant to the man who first spoke these words: Christ's death worked in him that his life might work in his people. Let us take the words in their fullest meaning too. Let the triumph of the cross be the one object of our life. Let the triumph of the cross on Calvary be the ground and the strength, let its triumph throughout the world be the one object of our intercession. Let its work be our plea. Let its spirit be our inspiration. Let its aim be our aim and our prayer.

Chapter 16

The Cross Revealing God's Love

'Herein is love, not that we loved God, but that he loved us, and sent his Son to be the propitiation for our sins.' 1 John 4:10

In the universe there is nothing so wonderful, so beautiful, so blessed as the love of God. God is love. 'Love seeketh not its own.' It is the glory of the divine being that what he is and has is not for himself: as God he is the fountain of all life and goodness, and finds his glory and his delight in making his creatures blessed with his blessedness. In his love, he lives out his life in them; his love is this, that he gives himself to them and in them. The delight of the divine life is to love and give and bless. Man's sin and fall gave the opportunity for a new display of what love is. When man had taken up the position of a rebel and an enemy, God still loved him, and undertook to do all that was needed to save him, at whatever cost. Sin had brought man under God's righteous judgment, and under the power of death. To bear that judgment, to die and conquer that death, God gave up his own Son, even to the accursed death of the cross. Because he loved us, and longed to win us back to his love; because his love could not rest without having our hearts for its home, and our love to satisfy his heart; he spared not his own Son, but gave him up for us all. The cross is the proof of how God loves us, of how he longs that we should know and enjoy his love, of how he desires after our love.

We need to study the cross in this aspect. Its death is not only a judicial transaction, is not only the power of an everlasting redemption, but is all this just in virtue of being something far more. It is the revelation and establishment of an intensely personal relation between God and us. It tells us that God in heaven loves each of us personally with such a love, that he would rather let his Son die, than we should not know his love. It tells us that he would give any price for our love. The stupendous mystery of the cross – the beloved Son dying the accursed death in agony and darkness – is the proof and the measure of God's love. God loved the world so much.

It is the very nature of love that it longs to make itself known, that it longs to possess the beloved object, that it cannot rest till it has won the heart and received its love in return. Think now of God in his inconceivable glory having condemned the sinner, yet giving his Son to bear that condemnation for those who hated and crucified him, and say – Is this not a love that passeth knowledge? And it is this love that comes to us in the cross and asks whether we have received it in its divine and inconceivable blessedness into our hearts, whether we are living and delighting in it, whether it has become, as such a God and such a love dare claim, the one desire and the one joy of our heart.

How incomprehensible the reception that love has met with. I speak not of those who reject it, but of those

who have believed in it, and professed to receive it. How
few there are who delight in it. How few who have given
up their whole life to it, to please it and tell out its wonders. How few to whom it is the chief joy of daily life that
the infinite love is on them and in them, and who would
suffer anything rather than grieve it. How few, even
among those who earnestly long for it, can testify that
the love has manifested itself to them, and taken up its
abode in them.

There must be some reason for this. What can be the
reason that this divine love, so infinitely desirous to communicate itself and fill us with its blessedness, so
omnipotent to overcome every barrier, cannot find
access even to those who say they long and pray to be
filled with it? Alas, I fear that all the different answers
that may be given at last resolve themselves into this:
they seek for it in their own way and strength. They have
not learnt the lessons of the cross: death to all that is of
nature, and natural power. They seek with the mind to
grasp as much as they can of this wonderful love, and
then by reflexion and argument to stir themselves to
love, in the hope of producing some impression that will
abide. And they never learn the lesson that as nothing
less than the death of the cross could reveal the love on
earth, so nothing less than that death working in the
heart, and bringing us into the grave, of utter helplessness and impotence, can reveal the love within us. And
this because they do not understand that, as divine as is
the love, and its unsealing on Calvary, so directly divine
must be its communication to each individual soul.

Come and listen while I seek to tell once again, as
simply as possible, what the path is in which God can see
the desire of his heart fulfilled, and the soul be brought
to live as he would have it, under the power of divine
love.

1. Begin with the cross; come and bow, and learn here
the double lesson of your utter impotence to grasp or
receive this love in its fullness, and the infinite willingness of God to give it in you.

Death to all self-will and self-effort, death to all that is of nature and the natural life, because it is sinful, and impotent of what is divinely good: this is the meaning of the cross. This is one of the reasons why the love of Christ could find no other way of leading us in the path of his salvation, than through the impotence of death and the grave: only in the utter despair and death of self can true love win and fill our heart. As the cross shows us what our nature is, and leads in perfect helplessness to cease from seeking in ourselves the power to receive or return this love, its first work is done: to turn from self is the first step in the path of love.

Those who thus despair of themselves will be prepared to receive the message the cross brings of God's infinite desire, at any price, to win our heart, and fill it with his love. In the cross we begin to see how God yearns for us, how he longs that we should know his love, and how sure it is that he himself will fill us with it.

2. As you then bow in the sense of your impotence and God's infinite longing to fill you with his love, believe in the Holy Spirit through whom the work is to be done. Love only began its work on the cross; it could not rest content till it was completed by the Holy Spirit coming down into the heart, and shedding abroad God's love there. It was the heart God's love wanted to win: the Spirit entered the heart to dwell there as the Spirit of love. Pentecost was the perfect triumph of the love of the cross in the hearts of the disciples. The cross reveals the love in its work for us; the Holy Spirit is the love dwelling in us and becoming our very life.

To each believer the Holy Spirit comes in regeneration as an earnest or first fruits of what will come. The fruit of the Spirit is love: learn to yield yourself in faith to his leading, and he can prepare you for a time when the full birth of the Spirit of love in the heart makes you know the love which passeth knowledge, so that you be filled with all the fullness of God.

3. Remember the price to be paid for this pearl of great price. The cross says what that price is. Eternal

love could find no way of casting out what is not love, no
way for love to triumph and open the way for us into all
God's love, but by giving up and forsaking all. It is
difficult to make it clear in words how absolutely, if this
divine life of love is really to possess and fill and rule over
all in us, everything of the material life must be hated
and lost. Things that appear most lawful, that appear to
be a duty, have to give way, if the infinite love is to have
sole and complete possession. The agony and death
struggle in which love won its victory, still comes, under
different forms, to demand our life at any cost. A heart
that has truly seen love in its divine beauty is ready to
turn from everything, that God's love may enter and
abide. Love and the cross are inseparably and eternally
linked. Seek the love: it leads you to the cross and its
death. Seek the cross: it leads you to love and its joy.

4. The cross is the measure of God's infinite desire that
we should know his love; if you would indeed receive
and enjoy it, seek for it with the desire of your whole
heart. 'They had sought him with their whole desire, and
he was found of them.'

Fix your desire on it, until it grows to a thirst that nothing can quench. Set your heart on the wonderful love
and the complete redemption the cross reveals. There is
nothing so wonderful, so strong, so beautiful, so blessed
as the love of God. This is the one thing in the universe
really worth knowing and possessing. God's love longs
exceedingly that it should have your heart and fill it. The
cross has removed every barrier out of the way of love
finding and filling you. It has opened heaven for the love
to flow out freely; it can open your heart for the love to
flow in fully. On the cross God proved that with his
whole heart he desired that his love should live in you by
giving his Son. Will you not with your whole heart desire
and plead for this blessing of blessings?

'Herein is love ... that he loved us, and sent his Son to
be the propitiation for our sins.' As wonderful and
divine as was the sending of the Son, as wonderful and
complete as his propitiation on the cross, so wonderful

and complete can be the entrance of his love into our hearts by the power of the Holy Spirit. God's love longs for this. Let us long and look for it. Let our faith in the cross with its atonement and its fellowship ever strengthen us to know perfectly the mystery it reveals: Herein is love, and let us not rest till that love has, within our heart, triumphed over all, and reigned alone.

Chapter 17

The Cross Inspiring Our Love

'Herein is love, not that we loved God, but that he loved us, and sent his Son to be the propitiation for our sins. Beloved, if God so loved us, we ought also to love one another ... If we love one another, God dwelleth in us, and his love is perfected in us.' 1 John 4:10–12

God's love to us, and our love to God and our neighbour, is one love. Love is the divine nature: when his love is shed abroad in our hearts, this is simply a new measure or power of the divine life taking possession of us. This love of God is in its nature unchangeable. As in God, so in us, it is a nature that delights in loving. It can do nothing else, it loves as naturally and unceasingly as the sun shines. God's love to us is set before us first as the obligation and the motive to love him and to love one another. As we seek to comply with this duty, and discover the selfishness and sin that makes it impossible, we are led on to see that God's love to us dwelling in the heart is alone the power by which we can love. And we understand how the word, 'We love him because he first loved us,' not only speaks of a motive, but of a living power his love brought into us. And how 'If we love one another' there is the proof, 'God dwelleth in us.'

The cross is the revelation and communication of the love with which God loves us. In virtue of this it is the inspiration of the love by which we love him with our whole heart and our neighbour as ourself. Let us study this. As the cross is seen to be in Jesus the death-blow to the natural life, the death to self-will, the death to sin and self, we shall see what is needed to make love in us the spontaneous and joyful outflow of a new nature. Christ could not find a pathway for the triumph of God's love but through the death of the cross, it is only the real and intimate fellowship of that death that enables us to love. The cross, received into the heart, inspires us with love.

1. The cross inspires us with love to God. Let me say again – not merely as a motive. All admit that we ought to love God who has so loved us: that gratitude ought to compel love. But it does not do so. A motive may stir a strong desire, but it cannot give the power. If our love of God is to be what he asks, the joyful love of the whole heart, the cross must do more than the law did. The law claimed it, because God had redeemed Israel out of Egypt, but did not give the life of love. Multiply that claim a thousandfold as you point to the greater redemption of the cross, you do not by that give the power to obey. The cross not only inspires the desire and the motive to love, but the very life that can love, the very love that cannot help loving.

The love of God did not reveal itself in the cross that we might from afar behold its beauty, and thirst to drink to the full of its streams, and then to rest content with such feeble experiences of it as our thoughts could apprehend. No. The love of God can be satisfied with nothing less than our heart as its home and its 'This is my rest for ever: here will I dwell; for I have desired it' (Compare John 14:21–23). God's love not only manifests itself on the cross to mankind as a whole: the cross brings a personal salvation; he waits to reveal his love in us. On the cross Christ so triumphed over all the powers of darkness that his redeemed can be set free from the dominion of sin and be made the actual recipients of God's holy love in their hearts.

It is only another aspect of the same truth when we say, On the cross our old man was crucified with Christ and we died to sin, to the old life of self and selfishness. Through that death we passed with Christ into his life unto God: the life of love takes the place of the life of self. 'In that he liveth, he liveth unto God.' 'I am dead unto the law, that I might live unto God.' 'Reckon yourselves to be alive unto God in Christ Jesus.' The life unto God is no other than a life that rises to him in love. Do let us believe it – the setting free from sin and self, the entering in of the life and love of God into the heart makes it possible to love God with all the heart. The cross not only shows but gives us his love in us.

2. The cross inspires us with love of the brethren. We have already seen that divine love, whether in God or in us, delights in loving, because it is its very nature. Like the sun, it shines on good and evil. From the heart of the believer it flows out, as having come from God on all who are born of God. 'Everyone that loveth him that begat, loveth also him that is begotten of him.'

The cross gives this power to love. How could he do otherwise who can say, 'I have been crucified with Christ'? There he not only had fellowship with Christ, but with all his fellow-redeemed, who were with him made partakers of the death and life and love of Christ. There he saw God in Christ taking them all together into his wonderful love: he knew them as the beloved of God. The cross has made an end of self and selfishness, and will he who is crucified with Christ not love them who all

bear the mark of the love of the cross? The cross con-
strains us to love.

How is it that this love is little seen and proved
throughout the church of Christ? There can be but one
answer. Because the cross is so little known as the one
law of our conduct, the one power of our life; because we
so little seek to be conformed to its death, the death of
love giving itself for all. We have gloried in the cross that
has atoned for sin, and reconciled us to God, and secured our peace. We have not, like Paul, gloried in the
cross by which we are crucified to the world and its self-
pleasing, on which we have crucified the flesh with its
every lust, through which we no longer live but Christ in
us. Oh let us beseech God to teach us that the cross is
love – God's love to us and our brethren, conquering and
possessing and inspiring us, and making us love one
another, even as Christ loved us.

3. The cross inspires the love of our neighbour. The
cross is love to the unworthy and to enemies: as
redeemed by the cross my love may know no other law.
The second commandment is like unto the first: Love the
Lord thy God with all thy heart is not more divine than,
Love thy neighbour as thyself. From the very com-
mencement of his ministry on earth, in the Sermon on
the Mount, he spoke of this as the mark of the kingdom,
the likeness of God's children to their Father in heaven.
Love to enemies, to the unthankful and the evil, is what
we are to do 'more than others.' Every prayer for mercy
is to be a plea that we forgive, even as our Father for-
gives us. The love of the cross was Christ's fulfilment of
his own commands to us: it makes love to enemies the
condition of partnership with its salvation.

What a test of the Christian life this call to love is. How
often when we are not on our guard, and meet unexpec-
tedly with disagreeable or provoking people, ungrateful
or worthless people, we give way to thoughts and feelings, to words and deeds that do not breathe the spirit of
the cross, the spirit of the love that asks not for worth or
reward but simply lives unto the death because it has

received and carries the love of God.

You doubt whether this is possible? Is it an ideal or a practical aim we seek to attain? 'The things that are impossible with men are possible with God.' Study again the cross to learn to believe that it is possible for love to love the vilest. It is possible for love to triumph over all the power of sin around thee and in thee. It is possible for the Holy Spirit, in a way above all that sense and reason can apprehend, to reveal and give the love of Christ into our hearts. It is possible, in one measure, to love as Jesus loved.

4. The cross inspires and empowers for the love of the whole world. The cross proclaims salvation to all, for – God so loved the world. Christ is a propitiation for our sins, and not for ours only, but also for the whole world. Jesus went from the cross to the throne saying: Preach the gospel to every creature. The love of the cross reaches out to all men: when it enters our heart, it commits us to loving all, and claims that our whole body, which it has redeemed, shall be yielded to the service of that love. The love the cross brings to us may have no aim lower than what it has prepared: 'I, when I am lifted up, will draw all men unto me.'

We speak of the missionary problem. Unceasing complaints are heard about the lack of interest and prayer, of men and money. Every possible device is restored to, to coax or to shame Christians into liberality. From every mission field there comes the story of the need for hundreds of more labourers if the work is to be done. Every society repeats the truth that if the churches would but wake up and accept their calling, the open doors and in many cases the hungry hearts are the pledge that God would open the windows of heaven, and pour down his blessing.

What does all this mean? That Christians have accepted the cross for a selfish salvation, with only so much of sacrifice for Christ as it pleases them to give, and does not cost them too much. They do not know that as absolute in its self-sacrifice as is the love which the cross reveals, is the love it seeks to bring and breath into our hearts. What the church needs is to be brought back to the cross, to learn not only the precious lesson of the great atonement, not only to learn the deeper lesson of fellowship in its crucifixion and death, but above all the highest lesson, that the love of the cross inspires and enables us, like Christ, to give our lives for the salvation of men. Let all who pray to God for the extension of his kingdom in the world make it their prayer, that the full light of the cross may shine into the heart of every believer, in all its power may work with his will, and the love that meant it for all the world becomes the law of our life.

Your Lord on the cross is the crucified love. Worship before him until the infinite love of God to you, and the wonderful passion of that love revealed in Christ takes possession of you. Worship before him until you have seen that love embracing every human creature with you. Worship still, until that love has become in your heart too the sacrifice and the death of all else for the joy of loving and saving souls. And worship still again, until that love gives you the power to impart the very love of God to those for whom it yearns.

Chapter 18

The Two Aspects of the Cross

'Who his own self bare our sins in his own body on the tree, that we, being dead to sins, should live unto righteousness.' 1 Peter 2:24

In the teaching of Scripture the cross is presented under two different aspects. In the words of Peter here we have them both. 'Christ, his own self bare our sins in his own body on the tree.' He did what we ought to have done, to bear the punishment and the curse of our sins. He did what we never could have done. He did what we now need never do. He died in our stead, and as our substitute, actually standing in our place, fulfilling for us every obligation to the law under which we were, and forever freeing us from it. The cross preaches the blessed truth of substitution – the Saviour taking the sinner's place, that now the sinner may share the Saviour's place.

This is the one side of the truth. Then comes the other, when we ask what is to be the result or fruit of Christ thus bearing our sins. The ordinary answer is, that we may now have our sins pardoned. This answer is according to Scripture. But it is only a part of scriptural truth. The answer Peter gives is: 'That we, being dead to sins, should live to righteousness.' The death of Christ is not only a death for us, a curse-bearing on the tree in which we can have no share, but equally a death in which we have an actual part, a death through which we die unto sin and enter a new life; all as really and truly as Christ did. Scripture equally teaches the substitution and the fellowship of the cross. The substitution of the cross, Christ dying for me the accursed death that I need not die it: the fellowship of the cross, Christ dying the death of the cross that I may die with him unto sin: such are the two blessed truths through which we enter into the full blessing of the cross of Christ.

We need to be very watchful lest we sacrifice either of these two truths to the other. There have been in all ages those who have sought to preach the fellowship of the cross without sufficiently presenting its substitution. The consequence was that men were led to seek their peace in the measure in which they thought that fellowship had been attained, and never came to know that perfect peace into which the sinner can enter at once when he trusts the finished work of his substitute. In our day the truth of substitution is overlooked or denied from another side. From false or defective views of the righteousness of God, the word of God: 'Christ hath redeemed us from the curse, being made a curse for us,' is set aside, and exclusive prominence given to what is called his love. On the strength of Christ's union with the human race in his incarnation, the thought of fellowship with him in his cross is so one-sidedly pressed, that the blessed foundation truth of his work of atonement, finished once and for ever, as the only and the sure ground of the sinner's acceptance, is overlooked or rejected. And the result is, just as in the other case, that men profess to believe in the cross, without ever learning there the lesson of their utter guilt and condemnation, or of the free and immediate and full acceptance into God's favour of which the cross assures. Oh for messengers of the cross who preach its substitution as the only and everlasting power of God unto salvation.

Let me therefore say here, for the sake even of a single reader who may yet be in the dark, see whether the reason that all your efforts to follow Christ and bear the cross, all your desires to live a holy life, have so failed, may not be for this reason: that you never have been led by the Holy Spirit to see how completely Christ, as your substitute, has borne your sins, has put away sin from between God and you, and what a full liberty of access you can at once have into God's love the moment you trust this Christ. Let the death of Christ, let the blood shed for the remission of your sins, let the peace which has been made by the blood of his cross, be your one confidence. This will be the beginning of new life to you. The substitution of the cross is the only door to its fellowship.

The opposite error is that of neglecting the fellowship of the cross in the too exclusive holding of the substitution. This is the danger to which those are specially exposed who seek to be most faithful to reformation doctrine. They know how the great reformation truth of justification and faith, and all the mighty blessing it brought the church, is inseparably linked to the blessed truth of substitution. They have seen what wonderful power it has to convince of sin and helplessness, and to bring peace to the troubled heart. They have observed how much just where the truth was neglected, the fellowship of the cross was vainly sought as the ground of peace or joy. They are sure that in it they have the very foundation of our salvation, and their faith and teaching have almost exclusive reference to it. The fellowship of the cross, our being crucified with Christ, the crucifixion of the old man, and the flesh, and the world, has not found the place in their system which it has in God's Word.

The harm that is done by their neglect of the fellowship of the cross is greater than is thought. It is one great cause of the feebleness and worldliness of the church. Men are not taught, definitely and persistently, that crucifixion as such is the great mark of the believer as of Christ; that crucifixion to the world, entire separation from it, regarding ourselves and it, like Paul, as crucified to each other, is the only power for victory over it, for proving that we are 'not of the world even as Christ was not of the world.' That the crucifixion of the flesh, and all that is of it, maintained daily in the power of the Holy Spirit, is essential to a holy life. That death to all that is of nature, natural goodness and natural strength, a daily dying and a bearing in the body the dying of the Lord Jesus, is the sure way to have the life of Jesus manifested in us. It was through the cross, with all that it implies in disposition and experience, that Christ entered his resurrection life, and his glory, and received from the Father the Holy Spirit to pour down. It is only through fellowship of the cross, with all that that implies in our disposition and experience, that we can come into the power of the Spirit. It is in the death to sin, and to the whole of that nature which is all tainted by sin, that we can enter into the full life of God. There are tens of thousands most earnestly pleading for the power of God's Holy Spirit in the church, and wondering that the answer does not come in greater power. We have reason to wonder. Our disappointment is not unreasonable. Let us see whether we have not been separating fellowship in the death of our crucified Lord, from our participation in his risen power, the life of the cross from the life of the Spirit. There is no entrance, personally and practically into the power of the heavenly life, no way to have the heavenly kingdom revealed within us as a personal enjoyment and possession, but by the full acceptance, in personal experience and manifestation, of the fellowship of the cross. Oh for me to preach, or rather, to practise and prove, and then to preach, the power and the blessedness of conformity to the death, to the cross, of

Christ Jesus our Lord.

Just notice the relation of these two aspects of the cross in the teaching of Peter. Both the remarkable passages referring to Christ's atonement for us are introduced, as it were incidentally, while he is speaking of the imitation of Christ as our example, and our fellowship in his sufferings. In 2:21 we read: 'Hereunto – that is, in patient suffering – were ye called: because Christ also suffered for us, leaving us an example.' And then, after reminding them what that example was, he continues: 'Who his own self bare our sins in his own body on the tree, that we, being dead to sins, should live to righteousness.' His death is at once our death to sin, our new life, and the power to suffer even as he suffered. The cross is at once his victory over the guilt of sin, and our victory over its power. And just so in chapter 3:14–17, after speaking of suffering for righteousness sake, he says: 'For Christ also hath once suffered for sins, the just for the unjust,' and then adds (4:1): 'Forasmuch then as Christ hath suffered for us in the flesh, arm yourselves likewise with the same mind: for he that hath suffered in the flesh hath ceased from sin.' There would be no force in the argument from Christ's example were it not for our union with him: in that union we find the double blessing: the immediate removal of guilt and dominion of sin, and the power, as dead to sin, to live unto righteousness. The atonement of the cross opens the gate into the new and living way; the fellowship of the cross marks our whole walk in that way. Even as its death to sin is Christ's entrance on the life to God, it is our only strength for the maintenance of that life.

What God hath joined, let no man put asunder. Have you not often wondered why the faith in the wondrous grace of the cross, with its atonement and acceptance so complete, does not stir more effectually to devotion and holiness? The reason is, most probably, you had not been taught that the fellowship of the cross is God's unchangeable demand, your highest privilege, and the secret power of the spiritual life. Throughout the church one hears scriptural preaching and sees Christian living, in which the conformity to Christ's crucifixion to the world is scarcely thought of. If God is indeed to visit his church, if there is to be a revival of spiritual living among believers, if the church is to be filled with the Spirit, so as to have the will and the power to live wholly for God and perishing men, our death with Christ to sin and the world will need to take a very different place to what it has had. It was the suffering and death of the cross that prepared Christ for receiving the Spirit from the Father. It was the disciples' fellowship with him through all that suffering and death that prepared them for receiving that suffering and death. It will be only fellowship with the crucified One that will prepare us for being filled with the Spirit too.

Chapter 19

The Cross and
the Living Christ

*'Fear not ye: for I know that ye seek Jesus,
which was crucified. He is not here: for he is
risen, as he said.'* Matthew 28:5–6

*'I am he that liveth, and was dead; and
behold, I am alive for evermore, Amen.'*
Revelation 1:18

The crucified Christ is now, and ever, the living Christ. The living Christ is still and ever, he that was crucified. The two sides of the truth must ever be held in their blessed unity. Without the death there never had been the resurrection life: without the cross, and its shame, there could never have been the throne and its glory. And so without the life, the death had brought no profit: it was only as the glorified one who gives the Spirit, that the crucified

Christ could save. Christ is he that was dead, and is now alive for evermore.

Even as these two are united in Christ, we need to hold both first in our knowledge and experience. The lack of insight into the meaning of, and surrender to, the power of the cross, must make our experience of the life defective. The attempt to believe in the cross, to bear it, and know all its wondrous saving power will equally fail, except it all be sought in the faith and the joy of a living Saviour and his personal love and fellowship.

The story of the resurrection morning suggests to us the danger of the latter of these errors – seeking the crucified among the dead, owing to ignorance or unbelief or forgetfulness that he is the living One. With what intense love the disciples clung to the crucified Lord: even his death made no difference. How blessed had been their fellowship with him: with what divine power had he worked in them and bound them to him: the cross had shattered all their hopes, but not torn their hearts from him. But, alas, their love only made the sorrow of the cross all the more bitter: its blessing and comfort they could not know till they knew that Jesus lived.

It has been so in all ages. How often the atonement of the cross has been preached and believed without it bringing the joy and the strength of the life which it was meant God to give. The truth of a living Saviour in heaven, dwelling in the heart, and himself communicating and maintaining the joy of a full forgiveness and a perfect redemption, was not given the place it ought to have. The soul struggles to trust in the work the cross has done, and to appropriate the blessings it promises, without knowing that all the dying Christ won for us, the risen Christ lives to impart to us in heavenly power. It seeks after and clings to the crucified One without the joy of his living fellowship and inworking.

And even so the fellowship of the cross has often become a burden and a penance, because souls were not pointed to the living one. When Christ said of his disciple 'let him take up his cross,' he at once added, 'and follow

me.' Without his living lead and love, there could not be
the power to bear the cross. Men have taught that we
must crucify ourselves and our lusts: Paul said 'I have
been crucified – with Christ – who lives – in me.' It was
because the living Christ gave in him his crucifixion
spirit, and himself made the cross the means of ever-
growing fellowship, and conformity, that Paul could
glory in it. The doctrine of the cross, meant of God to do
away with all self-righteousness, became its greatest
stronghold, as men sought, apart from the faith in a living Christ, to imitate its sufferings, or to reproduce its
self-sacrifice. With intense earnestness, with fervent
love, many made the great mistake of the disciples. They
sought him who is now the living One, among the dead,
in the grave.

In this book I am pleading for a larger place in our
Christian teaching and life to be given to the fellowship
of the cross. I have said that it is the one great need of the
church, in its pursuit of personal holiness, in its witness
to the world, in its preaching of the Gospel to saints and
sinners. I cannot too pressingly urge every believer to
ask and wait on God's Holy Spirit to reveal and to work
within him the fullest possible conformity to his crucified
Lord. Nothing less than this will make the presence of
the church in the world and its preaching a power of God
unto salvation. But now, just because I do see and urge
the need of knowing, in spiritual, experimental power,
nothing but Christ and him crucified, I want to point out
the one great danger against which we must be on our
guard. The fellowship and conformity of the cross is only
possible in the indwelling power of a living Lord. Where
Christ's living presence is not enjoyed, we seek in vain to
share his crucifixion spirit and power. When Christ is
known in his fullness the power of his crucifixion will
work spontaneously, almost unconsciously. When simple souls have loved their Lord intensely the spirit of his
cross has possessed them, and led them into his humility
and self-sacrifice, without their thinking much about
them being crucified with him.

The question may be asked: If this be so, is it not best to point directly to Christ as the living One, leaving him to teach what each needs about his cross? Our experience in natural life will give us the answer. Healthy men may breathe the air and eat their food, without knowing anything of their composition or the ways through which they do their work. It is disease that makes it needful for us to know what the elements and the proportions are that are required for pure air and wholesome food, and what the conditions on which the organs of respiration and digestion can duly fulfil their functions. In health the enjoyment of a blessing far exceeds our knowledge, and we suffer no loss. In sickness we know far more than we have; we need the knowledge now to regain what we have lost. Even so, where there is a healthy Christian life, where the Spirit is working in power, where we have the living Christ dwelling in the heart, he will give and work in us what we need, far beyond what we know or need to know. But where the church or the believer is in a sickly state, there the first need is to have the evil that is hindering discovered, the point at which it found entrance traced, and the special element that is lacking to build up a healthy life made clear. Only as this is seen and accepted, can the church come to the right apprehension of what has been lacking in its understanding of Christ, and what is needed for its restoration to the place from which it has fallen.

It is not so many years ago since the preaching of the resurrection life came to many almost like a new revelation. The message of a living Christ to be ever with us, to do all for us, himself to be our salvation and surety that all his cross had won should be ours, filled the heart with a joy and hope unknown before. And yet the hope was not always realised. Especially not the hope of a new and larger power in the battle with the powers of the world, and the effort to rescue men from its dominion. And the question has arisen, What is it that hinders the power of our faith in him whom we know to be the living and glorified one? Every answer, in whatever different shape it comes, points back to some form in which the spirit of the world secretly asserts itself. And to many earnest hearts the thought is coming, May it not be that the only way, the divine way, in which the world can be conquered has been forgotten – the way of the cross, 'by which the world is crucified unto me and I unto the world.' Christ crucified is the power of God. When his disciples take the stand Paul took: when they meet the world with the plain declaration: We ask you to regard us as men whom, in our Lord, you have crucified, who are now crucified to you, and whose glory it is that they are crucified with him, the power that wrought with Paul may be expected to work in us.

All the nature of a tree gathers itself up and reveals itself in every fruit. When that fruit becomes a seed, all the nature of the tree that was hidden in it is again manifested in its growth. The cross is the perfect fruit borne of Christ's life and spirit, giving the most perfect revelation of what he was. When the cross becomes the seed of life in our hearts, it begets a life and produces a growth exactly corresponding to that from which it has in its origin. In other words, when the living Christ is begotten and formed within us, his one aim is to transform us from our conformity to the world into his own likeness and image, and specially unto that which is his special glory, the spirit that shewed itself in his suffering and crucifixion. The atonement of the cross simply brings us into that relation to God and Christ, in which Christ can now effectually do his work, and conform us to himself and his cross.

The cross was God's thought: the cross came from heaven: it was through God's power and Spirit Christ bore it. There is nothing in the universe more divine than the cross. Nothing less than the power and Spirit of God can reveal the cross in us, or make us partakers of its inner mystery. It is this God who will work in us through the living Christ on the throne. Let us cease from every attempt to seek the crucified One or his fellowship among the dead in our own efforts or struggles after his imitation. Let us learn to look at the cross as the most divine of all that is divine in Christ, the greatest mystery of divine wisdom in him who is the wisdom of God, and therefore the most blessed part of all he has to teach or give us. We have yielded ourselves in resurrection joy to our living Lord: when we hear the call to the cross, let it, so far from leading us from him, draw us all the closer to him. Calvary is the inmost sanctuary in the life of Christ; his death the very gate of his glory. Let us yield ourselves to him who was dead and lives for evermore to impart to us in full measure the double blessing, never to be separated: a life in which the power of death to sin and the world ever works, and a death which is ever the entrance into a deeper life.

The Baptism of Fire

Chapter 1

The Fire and the Blessing it Brings

'And there came forth fire from before the Lord (at the dedication of the tabernacle), and consumed upon the altar the burnt offering.' Leviticus 9:24

'And David built there (on Morijah) an altar unto the Lord, and offered burnt offerings ... and called upon the Lord; and he answered him from heaven by fire upon the altar ... Then David said, This is the house of the Lord God.' 1 Chronicles 21:26; 22:1.

'Now when Solomon had made an end of praying, the fire came down from heaven, and consumed the burnt offering ... and the glory of the Lord filled the house.'
2 Chronicles 7:1.

*'And Elijah said: The God that answereth by
fire, let him be God ... Then the fire of the
Lord fell, and consumed the burnt offering,
and the wood, and the stones, and the dust,
and licked up the water that was in the trench.'*
1 Kings 18:24–38

Just those four times we read of heaven being opened,
and fire descending upon sacrifices laid upon the altar
before the Lord. As a token of his acceptance of the sacrifice, and his approval of the worshippers, as the answer
to their prayer, as the power by which the dead offering
was transformed into bright living flame rising heavenwards, it made man fall down and worship before the
Lord. To any of the hearers of John the Baptist, wondering what the Baptism of Fire might be, and looking to the
Old Testament for some clue to the meaning, there was
nothing so likely to suggest itself as the thought of the
burnt offering on the altar baptised, permeated with fire
from God in heaven, wholly possessed and consumed,
and by it carried heavenwards. Though we live in the full
light of the fulfilment of John's proclamation, the study
of the type will make clear to us some of the most precious lessons we need to learn.

Let us look first at the wonderful blessings this fire
from heaven on the altar brought. It was a sign of
immediate communication between earth and heaven, a
direct revelation of the presence and favour of God. In
every sacrifice, even when the fire for it has to be made
here on earth, there was communion with God. But in
the four instances cited God met special need with the
special token of his favour, and the special manifestation
of himself as the God whom they were seeking.

Hence we read of the dedication of the tabernacle:

'And when all the people saw it, they shouted, and fell on their faces.' When the fire fell on Moriah to consume David's sacrifice, he knew that this was to be the place for the house of the Lord: the fire was the sign that God had come to dwell there. Of the dedication of the temple when the fire had come down, we read: 'The glory of the Lord filled the house. And the priests could not enter into the house of the Lord, because the glory of the Lord had filled the Lord's house. And when the children of Israel saw how the fire came down, and the glory of the Lord upon the house, they bowed themselves with their faces to the ground and worshipped, and praised the Lord, saying, 'For he is good; for his mercy endureth for ever.' And on Carmel, when the fire of the Lord fell, and all the people saw it, they fell on their faces and said: 'The Lord, he is God; the Lord, he is God.' In each case the Baptism of Fire brought the direct overwhelming proof of the presence and glory of God. At other times they might doubt, or fear, or forget: the fire from heaven was the irresistible evidence that God was there.

And is not just this the need of our Christianity in these our days – the presence of God truly revealed and felt? And is it not just this for which the Baptism of Fire was promised, and is so indispensable? In John's Baptism there were indeed tokens of God's presence and power. He could testify that God had sent him. He could hold forth the wonderful promise of the kingdom of heaven. He could with convincing power preach repentance and forgiveness. He could point to Jesus, on whom he had seen the Holy Spirit come down and abide, and who would baptize with the Holy Spirit and with fire. But more he could not do. He had been filled with the Spirit from his mother's womb, and there was a measure of the Spirit's power in his preaching. But with all this, the Baptism of Fire he could not give. Even Christ himself could not give it, until as a victim on the altar he himself had been consumed by the fire, and in that fire had been lifted up as a glorified One into heaven. When the Baptism of Fire came, was not its chief work the perfect consciousness that the fire had come from above, that it was God's fire renewing and filling the whole being with his presence? Without appealing to promise, or reflection, or argument, they knew and felt: this is God, this is God's Spirit filling us.

Just this is what many are longing for. The preaching of the Gospel is not without blessing and fruit: the operations of the Spirit are not unknown: but they hardly reach much beyond the power of the water-baptism: there is true repentance, and the joy of forgiveness, even as at Philip's preaching in Samaria. But there is something lacking. People remind themselves, or have to be reminded, as Paul did the Corinthians, that they have the Spirit. But the joyful assurance of Pentecost – I have received the Holy Spirit direct from the Lord in heaven: the fire of God has come and accepted and is consuming the sacrifice: the fire of heaven in my heart is the direct proof of God's presence in me – this is all too little kown. The Baptism of Fire is God's direct revelation of himself taking and holding and transforming the offered sacrifice for himself. The fire is the revelation of the holiness and glory of God taking possession of his temple. It will teach us to know the Holy Spirit as dwelling in us and keeping the divine life in us as simply and as naturally as we know that we are alive with the life of nature.

You cry, Oh to be thus baptized with the fire of God! To have the fire of heaven, with its refreshing, quickening, God-revealing and God-glorifying power, possess me all the day. You long to know how to attain this wonderful blessing. The Baptism of Fire on the burnt offering on the altar gives the answer. At the dedication to the tabernacle Moses had said (Lev 9:6): 'This is the thing which the Lord commanded that ye should do: and the glory of the Lord shall appear unto you.' The tabernacle had all been made 'as the Lord commanded'; the sacrifices were prepared according to God's will; the whole burnt offering was on the altar in token of entire consecration; all was surrendered: the fire came to claim and accept all. It was even so with David; when the burnt offering was prepared, he called upon the Lord. The fire came to consume the sacrifice: that was God's answer to his prayer. With Solomon, too, when he had made an end of praying, the fire came from heaven, and consumed the burnt offerings. It is ever the same: the fire demands a sacrifice: it must have its food: the fire from heaven only comes where everything on earth is prepared to yield to its all consuming power. It is a heart most completely, utterly, given up to God that can expect the Baptism of Fire.

See with what force this comes out in the case of the sacrifice of Elijah on Carmel. Notice first the prophet's entire isolation and separation from all around: 'I, even I only, remain a prophet of the Lord; but Baal's prophets are four hundred and fifty.' If you would have God answer you by fire, you must begin by entire and intense separation from all the worldly and half-hearted religion that surrounds you. You must come out as a man who stands up for God. Then see how 'he built an altar in the name of the Lord'; in his worship and his sacrifice, God, his will and his glory, is to be all. Mark how he had the altar and the sacrifice surrounded with water: his faith trusts God to manifest his mighty power; he counts upon the fire to overcome the greatest hindrances. Listen to him pleading with God, not for himself, but for God's honour, and for the deluded people. He calls for the fire that God may be known and the people brought back to his fear and service. Study all this and you will understand as you read, 'Then the fire of the Lord fell, and consumed the burnt sacrifice, and the wood, and the stones, and the dust, and licked up the water that was in the trench.' When everything is done as where Elijah prepared his sacrifice, the Baptism of Fire will surely come.

Oh, Christian friends, the unspeakable blessing of the pentecostal fire-baptism is ours, if we will but come to receive it in God's way. All these four witnesses teach us just one lesson: it is where everything is prepared to give God alone the honour, where everything is ordered in entire surrender to his demand, where 'the whole burnt offering on the altar' has been taken as a type of the absolute surrender of our life to the death, for God's Holy Spirit to receive it and consume it in his service, there the Baptism of Fire is sure to come. We have seen David, and Solomon, and Elijah, all praying and calling upon God to reveal himself: the prayer would not have been heard if the whole burnt offering had not been there waiting to be consumed. The fire from heaven is to turn the life of earth through death into the worship and the service of God.

Do let us believe that the Spirit and fire from heaven which John proclaimed are meant to make and keep us living sacrifices our whole life through, every day and every moment. We can have the fire of God burning through our whole being and all its powers, through our very bodies, making them living, holy and well pleasing sacrifices. It can be. It has been. It will be, to every one who is ready to give up all, to count all things but loss, to hate and lose his life that Christ may live in him. Christ took his disciples and prepared them for the fire baptism by training them three years in the following of his steps and the fellowship of his surrender to the Father. They clung to him as men who sought nothing but him alone; it could not be but that he filled them with his Spirit.

The path to the blessing lies clear and open before us: the whole burnt offering receives the Baptism of Fire. First a death, then the transfiguration the fire brings. It was so with Christ; it must be so with us. Are you ready for this? Possibly you feel as if you are not willing to give up all. Or as if, though you are willing, you do not know how it is to be done, what all it requires, whether you will have the power to fulfil it faithfully. Be of good cheer, I have a word of unspeakable comfort. God not only sent the fire from above; he ordained his servants to prepare the sacrifice. Aaron the priest, David the king, Elijah the prophet, laid the burnt offering on the altar in his name. Christ not only baptizes with the fire; he prepares the sacrifice. In Christ we not only find out all that God is to be to us; we find in him that we are to be God. He is our High Priest to bring us to God. Before he gave his disciples the promised Baptism of Fire he prepared them for it. Yield yourself to your Redeemer in the confident assurance that he will make thee partake of the Spirit and the power of his death; that he fits you then for the absolute surrender he asks. Yield yourself in the faith that the Baptism of Fire is for you. Wait on your ascended Lord and High Priest to work both in you, the blessed preparation of the sacrifice, the more blessed fulfilment of the promise: He shall baptize you with the Holy Ghost and with fire. And go out today and each day as one set apart, and accepted, expecting and receiving the fullness of the Spirit of God.

Chapter 2

The Two Baptisms: Their Resemblance

*'John answered, saying, I indeed baptize you
with water; but there cometh he that is
mightier than I ... he shall baptize you with
the Holy Ghost and with fire.'* Luke 3:16

Every symbol or type suggests both a resemblance and a
difference. It is through similarity that the outward and
visible can help us to form a better conception of the
invisible and spiritual. On the other hand it is by its contrast that the outward points to that which is higher and
alone has the true substance of which the type was but
the shadow and sign. When John places the two baptisms, the water baptism and the fire baptism, beside
each other, we need first to consider the likensss; then
we shall be better able to appreciate the glory that excelleth, the wonderful blessedness of the latter. We begin

today with the resemblance.

In either case it is a Baptism – an entering into an element that is to surround us and do its work in us. That is to be the pledge to us of something we need and seek. In either case there is a Baptist, to whom we have to draw near, with whom we have to come into personal contact, and who by Divine authority is to give us what we cannot take for ourselves. And in either case there is also a preparation that must precede – the Baptist's first work is to search the life and see if the heart is in a fit state for receiving what the Baptism is meant in God's name to give.

1. In either case there was a Baptism. John baptised with water. The idea was a very simple one. Water cleanses away defilement. The candidate for baptism came repenting of and confessing his sins, and seeking to be freed from them. The Baptist came preaching the forgiveness of sins, and the washing with water was to be a symbol of the removal of sin which forgiveness brings. In the Christian Church the baptism with water had a far deeper meaning, the entering the water being the symbol of being one with Christ in his death and burial, as the complete and perfect liberation from sin. For the multitudes on the banks of the Jordan this thought would have been far too deep. The baptism with water was the confession of their desire to put away their sin, of their faith in God that he did indeed put it away out of his sight.

Jesus was to baptise with fire. The thought was so new and wonderful, there was apparently nothing in the Old Testament to help the conception of a man being baptised in fire, that the only aid would be to look to the analogy of the water baptism. The thought would be suggested of sin being dealt with in a mightier and more effectual way than its mere forgiveness, as the water baptism had promised. The thought would come of a man's whole nature somehow being taken up into and entirely mastered by the heavenly fire of the Holy Spirit. It was meant to wake the heart to the expectation that

even as John, the man of earth, baptised with an element
of earth, so Jesus, who had himself just at his baptism
received the Holy Spirit direct from the Father in
heaven, would give to his disciples in such divine reality
as John could not, the power of the heavenly world for
their heart and life. The two baptisms would exactly cor-
respond as a shadow to its substance, as an image to its
original, as a promise to the thing possessed. The water
baptism was the initial rite admitting men to the earthly
discipleship of John and of Jesus in peparation for the
kingdom of heaven which was at hand. The Fire Baptism
was the initial rite admitting them to the full fellowship
of the kingdom of heaven come down and established in
their hearts.

2. In either case there was a Baptist, a servant
ordained by God to do the work. 'And there went out
unto him all the country of Judaea, and all they of
Jerusalem'; men had to leave their homes and friends to
come and receive from his hands what he alone could
give. If they did not believe in him; if they were too
proud and self-satisfied to bow to him; if they were too
indifferent to undertake the journey, they could not
share in what his baptism was meant to bring. Personal
contact with the Baptist was the first condition of the
Water Baptism.

It is not otherwise with the Fire Baptism. It is of
exceeding importance to understand this point of
resemblance. Earnest Christians are often found mourning the lack of the Baptism of Fire, and longing for it.
They read and listen to all that can help them towards it.
They are intently occupied in seeking to cultivate in their
own hearts, with prayer and the study of the Word, what
they think to be lacking. They pray very fervently at
times, but their prayers are far more the expression of
intense desire than of contact with Jesus Christ in trust-
ful faith and hope. The man who went from Jerusalem to
go to Jordan left his friends with the clear understanding
– I am going to John to be baptised. His first desire was
to see and hear and speak to John. John was known by

the name of John the Baptist. 'And there went out unto him all the country of Judaea ... and they were baptized of him.' Just as simple and natural ought to be the thought of each seeker after the Baptism of Fire. It is Jesus baptises with the Holy Spirit and with Fire. I will go to him to be baptised of him.

The thought is of such infinite consequence that I want at the very outset of our meditations to say to each reader: see that you fully master it – or rather that it gets full possession of you John preached Christ unto two titles. The one Jesus, the Lamb of God, who takes away the sins of the world, you know well. Your whole hope of salvation rests on it. The other is, Jesus the Baptist who baptises with the Holy Spirit and with Fire. Let this name be to you as precious as the other. Open your heart to it. Let your faith embrace it, and with it embrace him. Oh! let us begin our study and our quest of the Baptism of Fire with the simple, confident assurance. He does baptise with fire. As sure as John did his work, and never turned away one honest enquirer, so surely will Jesus do his. Let us praise him for it. Let us, all Jerusalem, go out unto him, to be baptised of him. God has not hid or withheld this blessing from us: as truly as John was sent into the land of Israel to do his work, Christ is ready to do his work in his church on earth.

3. The third point of resemblance is the preparation. John preached, repentance. They were baptised, confessing their sins. Without repentance and confession of sin there was no Water Baptism.

The same is true of Fire Baptism. Christ took the disciples out of John's school into his own, and for three years trained them for the Fire Baptism by the discovery of their hidden sinfulness. He showed them their lack of humility, and love, and self-denial, and faith. It was only after Peter had wept bitterly, and had confessed his love with sorrow at the thought of what a failure it had been, that he received this baptism. For the Fire Baptism Christ himself alone can prepare us.

There are so many Christians whose conviction of sin

when they received pardon was so feeble that before they can think of the Baptism of the Spirit, John's teaching is just what they need. Just notice its varied and searching and most personal application of the word repent. To the multitude he said: 'Bring forth fruits worthy of repentance, and begin not to say within yourselves, we have Abraham for our father.' Trust not in your privileges as God's people; trust not in your profession of repentance; bring forth fruits worthy of it. Let your holy life prove your sincerity. And when they asked: 'What shall we do?' his answer was 'He that hath two coats, let him impart to him that hath none.' Obey the law of love, prove thy repentance by a life of unselfishness and self-sacrifice. When the publicans came, his answer to their, 'And what must we do' was 'Exact no more than that which is appointed you.' Whatever loss it may entail, whatever others do, let strict honesty mark your conduct. And the demand of the soldiers he met as personally with his 'Do violence to no man, neither exact anything wrongfully; and be content with your wages.' Do justice, love mercy; without these there could be no thought of living in God's favour. Such was the path to the Water Baptism.

And the path to the Fire Baptism? It must begin here too. John preached repentance to those who sought baptism from him. Christ does the same. What we need when we come to him is to allow him to discover all the evil there is in us. We know how faithfully and graciously he did the work for his disciples. They could have passed John's examination. But Christ led them deeper. He dealt not with external things, but with the sins of the inner life, with the sinfulness of the flesh which the spirit, however willing, could not master. He gently and tenderly taught and guided them, until they had been brought to utter despair of themselves, and had nothing to hope in but his promises and power.

My dear Christian friends, the Water Baptism and the Fire Baptism deal with one evil – the evil of sin. They answer one question: How can I be delivered from sin?

The full, final answer they give is very different indeed. But the first part of their answer is the same; they both call aloud, Repent, confess, forsake sin. Give up every sin, John cries, I baptise you with water in token of the forgiveness of your sins. Give up every sin! Christ speaks in a far deeper sense: and I baptise you with the Spirit and Fire as the Power to deliver you from its rule. If you would indeed seek the Baptism of the Spirit, understand this: it is meant to deliver you fully from the power of sin, and you cannot receive it unless the desire to be freed from sin be strong and very honest. Some seek for the blessing for the sake of being happy, and some for the sake of being useful. They will be disappointed; God offers it for making us holy, of bringing us into perfect union with his will. He seeks to deliver us from our pride, and our selfishness, and to have Christ alone, in his love, live in us. If we seek above everything to be freed from our sin and to have the Baptism of the Spirit, that Christ and his will may have the complete mastery in us, if we seek it for the sake of God's holiness, that he may be glorified, and Christ be all, our happiness and our usefulness will come of themselves. May God help us to know, to confess, to hate, to give us all sin, that the Holy Spirit may fill us.

'I baptise with water; he that is mightier than I shall baptise you with the Holy Ghost and with fire.' Christ, the mighty One, we come unto thee, to be baptised of thee! We cling to thee, we trust in thee. Thou wilt begin and thou will complete. We believe with our whole heart in thee as him who baptiseth with the Holy Spirit and with fire.

Chapter 3

The Fire Kept Burning Continually

> '*And the fire upon the altar shall be kept burning thereon, it shall not go out; and the priest shall burn wood on it every morning.... Fire shall be kept burning upon the altar continually; it shall not go out.*
> Leviticus 6:12–13

In all religions there are two factors. God and man both work. He that knows aright the place God ought to have, and the place man has to take, has learnt one of the deepest secrets of the Christian life. It is not only that God is first and man second; but God is all. Man's work is to receive and respond to the divine working by his surrender and obedience to it. The fire on the altar came from heaven to earth. The fire on the altar had to be maintained and kept burning continually; this was man's work. When the believer has received the Baptism of Fire from on high the injunction is heard: the fire shall be kept burning continually: it shall not go out. The Baptism of Fire is to lead to a life of tender and diligent watchfulness, lest anything be allowed that could quench the Spirit. To realise the force of this let us look at the fire burning on the altar and answer these four questions: Where? Why? How? Who?

Where? On the altar. And what was the altar? For sinful man seeking his God, the very centre of worship: the place set apart from all the world around where man brought his sacrifice, and God signified his acceptance. And what is our altar? Christ is the altar that sanctifieth the gift. And then, when we have been accepted and sanctified on the altar, our heart in its turn becomes the altar on which the fire descends, and where it is to be kept burning continually.

The lesson is one of deep meaning. If the fire is to come to the sacrifice on the altar, it is then to be kept burning, prepared for every new sacrifice. There must be an altar, a separated, consecrated place, given up to this one thing – to be a place where the fire from heaven can be kept burning. Yes, believer, as entirely as the altar of old was given up to the fire to burn there without ceasing, thy heart is to be given up for the fire of God to burn there without intermission. If there is one thing that God asks it is the whole heart, a perfect heart, all the heart, and all the strength. If there is one thing Christians do not understand it is this: that God absolutely requires that the interest, and attention, and enthusiasm of our whole being are to be given up to seek his will and his favour. Men think this a hardship and an impossibility. They do not see that the claim is just, that God can ask nothing less; that the claim is most blessed, because it is the only way in which the God of infinite love and blessedness can fully communicate himself to us. Men think that it is not possible because they do not by faith see how the eternal God, when he by his Holy Spirit takes possession, brings a new life, and power, and joy, in presence of which the mountains flow down, and God is revealed as the mighty present power that fills and holds all.

Do let us grasp this very firmly: to keep the fire burning continually it needs an altar entirely given up to it. Let us say believingly: Every moment the fire from heaven can and will burn in my heart: I yield it and God takes possession.

2. The second question was, Why? Why should the fire be kept burning continually? In our hearths and furnaces we let the fires go out when their work is done. As long as there is need of them they are kept up. The fire on the altar of the heart cannot be kept burning continually merely as a duty, or a privilege. It is needed for the work to be done. And that work is to continue the sacrifices. The slain lamb or ox brought to the altar for a burnt offering would soon turn to corruption and become an offence: the fire takes it, and transforming it into its own light nature, lifts it in beautiful living flames heavenwards as a sweet-smelling savour. The dark dead thing of earth is by the fire changed into the brightness and the light of heaven.

It is for this the Baptism of Fire is given. Where it burns, and is kept burning on the altar, it takes our whole being, with its every power, and nature, and makes it an acceptable sacrifice. Every purpose, and every vow we make before God: every desire and every prayer we breathe: every act of devotion, or worship, or service – the fire turns it all into flames of love. Every conflict in which we wrestle with the Evil One, or with the evil around us: every service of patient love or earnest effort for our fellowmen; every gift, even to the widow's farthing, that humility lays at the feet of Jesus; the flame on the altar of the heart makes it a sweet-smelling savour. We are to glorify God in our bodies; Christ is to be magnified in our body whether by life or by death; the death and the life of Christ are to be manifested in our mortal body; it is the fire continually burning that can make every moment of our life a living sacrifice, holy, acceptable to the Lord.

Oh, the heavenliness of a life when the fire is always kept burning. Nothing can enable you, believer, to live the true life, the temple life, but the Baptism of Fire. Think of it no longer as the special privilege of a few. You need it absolutely to live continually well pleasing to your Father, and to have continually the consciousness of that good pleasure. The fire of heaven can effect this.

3. How? How is it to be done? How is the fire from heaven to be kept burning day and night? Listen to the command: 'The priest shall burn wood on it every morning.' What a combination of the heavenly and the earthly. The fire comes from the very throne of God; the dull, dark, dead wood of the earth will be its food. Even so it is the spiritual life. In Scripture we have the words of this earth, just like the words we use in daily life. In themselves they are without life or power: the mind can study, and master, and utter them, but they bring neither help nor blessing. 'The letter killeth.' 'It is the Spirit that quickeneth, the flesh profiteth nothing.' It is the fire of the Holy Spirit that takes them as its fuel, and makes them the power by which the fire is kept ever burning.

It is a terrible mistake to think that when once a man is filled with the Spirit, the quiet persistent study of God's Word, and the reverend whole-hearted submission to it, is not as much needed as before. There is an ever-increasing number of witnesses who testify to the absolute need of the precept: 'The priest shall burn wood on the altar every morning.' With each new morning the ashes were to be removed, the fire that had been burning all night was to be stirred, and fresh wood brought for the day's need. Without a time of quiet each morning, in which God's teaching is accepted afresh in the light and power of the Spirit, the fullness of blessing cannot be maintained.

The wood and the fire – let us learn how great the difference, how close the connection, how essential the dependence on each other. To enjoy the blessing they together bring be sure and take them as God has joined them together. Believe that the Father has given the Holy Spirit to be expounder of his Word to every child of his. If you are a child, as sure as you have the word in your mouth, you have the Spirit in your heart, as an earnest or first-fruits of his fullness. Seek to recognise by a quiet faith the Spirit as dwelling in your heart. Understand that it is in the heart the whole work of God is to be done. Before you read, prepare your heart; waken its hunger and thirst for God in his word. Speak to God: 'I delight to do thy will, O my God: yea, thy law is within my heart.' 'Consider how I love thy precepts.'

Be sure that the Spirit, as a hidden fire, will enlighten you, and count upon him to make the word, which will to your reason be but as a dead letter, life and spirit. In the faith you will have the courage for entire consecration – you will dare to say 'I have sworn and will perform, that I will keep thy righteous judgments.' You will feel that without this you dare not count upon the Spirit's teaching. The fire must not only have the wood as fuel, but must have a sacrifice; not only the Word, but absolute surrender to obey and to do. But you will feel that with this, the fire of God to lift the Word and the life heavenward, you dare say it. Meet and worship God each morning in his Word. Bow in holy surrender to all his will and wait on him, until your faith receives the fresh assurance: the fire of God is burning on the altar. And your confidence will be ever brighter: the fire can be kept burning continually.

4. Who? 'The priest shall burn the wood every morning.' No one can do priest's work unless he knows that he is a priest. Christ was the altar, and the sacrifice, and the Priest all in one. Even so the believer. His heart is the altar; his life is spirit, soul and body, the sacrifice; he himself the priest.

We know what a priest was. A man taken from out of his people, and entirely set apart to God for worship and service. Our priesthood as believers is as real, demands

as entire a consecration of our whole time and power as
that of the priest in Israel. The man who yields himself
whole-heartedly to this service, who seeks to be all
priest, and nothing but priest, is he who will have the
heart and the power to keep the fire burning continually.
He knows he can have it; he knows the blessedness of
seeing it carry every offering heavenward: 'the priest
shall burn the wood every morning.'

How this thought brings us once again to that which is
the central truth in the human aspect of the Baptism of
Fire: the need of absolute surrender, of entire consecration. What is the work of the fire? It claims the whole
being of which the heart is the centre, as the sacrifice it
waits to carry heavenward from morning to night. What
is the wood? It is the Word of God, accepted, delighted
in, and sworn to in willing surrender. And who is to keep
the fire burning? The man who knows that he has been
made a priest unto God, who knows himself to be wholly
God's, and to have but one work – to keep the fire burning continually all the day.

But can it really be? Can the Christian truly live thus?
We can. What we try to express in all these words comes
as a unity and reality to the soul that receives the Baptism of Fire. The thought may arise: But there is human
responsibility, and need of faithfulness; and does not the
failure come in there? O thou who art called a priest,
knowest thou not thy High Priest? As thou hast charge
of the fire, so he hath charge of thee. If thou wilt entrust
thy faithfulness to his, thine will be sure as his. It is he
who baptises with fire; it is he who from heaven keeps
the communication of the Holy Spirit evermore active
and fresh in unbroken continuity; it is he keeps thee
through the Spirit. Do let us believe that the Baptism of
Fire is the direct, mighty and abiding participation in the
Spirit and the life of Jesus: to the faith that obeys God's
Word it will be a fire that shall not go out.

Chapter 4

The Two Baptisms: Their Difference

*'Why baptisest thou, if thou art not the Christ?
… John answered, I baptise with water…. He
that sent me to baptise with water, he said unto
me, Upon whomsoever thou shalt see the
Spirit descending, and abiding upon him, the
same is he that baptiseth with the Holy Spirit.'*
John 1:25–33

We have seen the points of resemblance between the
two baptisms: let us now trace the difference. It is that
between earth and heaven: between man and God. In all
religion there is an earthly and a heavenly element: man
and God act together. But everything depends upon
which of these take the first place and which the second.
As long as earth and man take the first place, religion is
a feeble thing and a continual failure. When heaven and

God are first and do the work, our worship and our service stand in the power of God and the heavenly life. The Baptism of water was of the earth, earthly; the Baptism of Fire was of heaven, was divine. The more truly we enter into and realise the infinite distance, the brighter may our hope be of what the Baptism of Fire can do for us.

1. The Baptism of Fire gives the power of a heavenly life. The whole work of John the Baptist was to point away from himself to Christ. The same is the case with every servant of God, with the Word of God itself and every appointment of life: they first draw to themselves to give their message and do their work in us, and then end by telling that they cannot do for us what we need to seek, and by sending us away from themselves to the only One who can truly bless. This is pre-eminently the case with the Water Baptism. John spake: 'That he should be made manifest to Israel, therefore am I come baptising with water.' 'He must increase, but I must decrease. He that cometh from above is above all: he that is of the earth is earthly, and speaketh of the earth.' And the one mark he gave, by which Jesus was to be known, was this: 'He that sent me to baptize with water, the same said to unto me, Upon whom thou shalt see the Spirit descending, and remaining on him, the same is he which baptizeth with the Holy Ghost.'

John's baptism was the close of the long Old Testament series of carnal ordinances, 'which could not make him that did the service perfect, as regarding the conscience.' Water is the symbol of the Word of God and every outward means of grace. But we must be born 'of water and the Spirit.' The means of grace have a certain influence and power of blessing, in calling and helping men to repentance and hope of forgiveness. But they do not and they cannot bring the power of the heavenly world into the heart and inner life as actual possession and enjoyment. This Christ alone can do. He came from above, from heaven; He received the Spirit from the opened heaven, abiding upon him; he returned to heaven; from heaven, from the very throne of God he baptised with the Spirit and Fire of heaven. The work of John sought to reach the heart from without by thoughts and arguments, by the stirring of the will and affections. Christ took possession of the heart within by fire from the throne of God. The Water Baptism was earthly, and outward, and feeble; the Fire Baptism was heavenly, and inward, and almighty.

To illustrate the difference, think of what we see done at Johannesburg with the gold. When the ore has been crushed, water is turned on, in which it is stirred, until as much as possible of the earthly matter is separated. The gold sediment that is gathered is once again subjected to the cleansing of flowing water, and all the outward earth that clings to the gold is removed. But farther than this the water cleansing cannot go. The dross there may be within the little grain of gold the water cannot reach, for this the fire is needed. As the fire melts the gold the most secret particle of dross is discovered and brought out and removed, and the gold comes out of the fire pure and bright. What the water baptism with its external cleansing could not do for the gold, the fire baptism penetrating into its inmost being has done.

Alas, how little we believe in or realise the power and the glory of the Fire Baptism, ready to cleanse our whole inner being by filling it with the life and power of heaven. We think of its difference from the Water Baptism as only one of degree. And the difference is one of kind: the fire of God, the fire which is the life of him who is a consuming fire, the fire of God is what Christ baptiseth with. Even as beautiful flames on earth are nothing but the wood or coal transformed by the fire into its own light nature, so the fire of God cleanses and beautifies by filling the heart with its own heavenly glory.

2. Yes, the Fire Baptism works a transformation of character. The Water Baptism dealt with character too: it demanded repentance, and fruits worthy of repentance. John raised high the standard of godly living, and called to a life of righteousness and love, as what alone

could satisfy God. He sought to waken to stronger desire and effort after such a life, but the power to live truly he could not give. He pointed to the nearing kingdom of heaven as what would bring with it the power of a heavenly life. He pointed to Jesus who baptises with Spirit and Fire as the One who would give that power. And even so Jesus took his own disciples first to teach them, during their three years with him, what the graces were he would have them exhibit, and then to point them to himself when glorified, and to the Spirit he would give, as the power to be and do even as he had been and done. He taught them that meekness and lowliness of heart, self-denial and cross-bearing, humility and love, surrender to the life of a servant, even to the giving the life for others, were the spirit in which he had lived with them, and in which he wanted them to live like him. And he promised them the fire of heaven to consume the pride and the selfishness, the spirit of the world and of the flesh within them, and to make them one in him, even as he was one in the Father.

When the Fire Baptism came it proved that it was truly able to effect the entire transformation of character. The natural character did indeed retain its peculiar type: the three who formed the inner circle, Peter and James and John, still retained their place as leaders, each with his own peculiar temperament. But all was renewed and purified. It is the same gold that comes out of the furnace, but with the dross removed. After Pentecost it is still Peter and James and John, but pride and unlovingness have been consumed in the fire of God's love, and the thought of self, its honour and its will purged out in the fire of Christ's death on the cross. The Baptism of Fire has wrought a miracle for them: now they are indeed 'not of the world, even as Christ was not of the world.' Now they prove that his kingdom is not of the world. They have been taken up into the kingdom of heaven, where the fire of God's presence fills and glorifies all. They have had the kingdom of heaven come down and enter and dwell in them. The promise had been fulfilled in anticipation of the coming of the day of God, wherein the heavens being on fire shall be dissolved, and there shall come the new heaven and the new earth, wherein dwelleth righteousness.

The water baptism was a thing done once for all. The earthly fire baptism of gold is a thing done once for all. Both are subject to the conditions of time and place. In the eternal world everything acts in the power of an endless life, in the unbroken continuity, moment by moment, of the life of God. It is because the heavenly fire burns and can be counted on unceasingly, that the transformation of character can be permanent, and Peter and James and John, the fishermen of Galilee, could in their old age write the epistles they have left us. Oh, let us believe it: He baptises us with the Holy Spirit and with Fire, that our whole inner being may be filled with the very life of heaven, that our character and conduct may be the fellowship and reflection of his because we are indeed baptised with the very baptism wherewith he was baptised.

3. The fire baptism gives the endowment for service. Just look back again a moment to John's water baptism, and see how wonderfully the contrast brings out this thought. There the only thought was that of personal salvation. Men sought the forgiveness of their sins. There was not a word or a thought of their giving themselves to God's service in becoming messengers to others. How different with the fire baptism. On one of the few occasions when, during his public ministry, our Lord mentioned the Spirit, it was to say that when they were brought before councils and kings they were to take no thought: 'for it is not ye who speak, but the Spirit of your Father which speaketh in you.' In his farewell discourse how distinctly our Lord told them: 'The Spirit shall bear witness and ye shall bear witness.' And in parting with them at the Ascension the one thought was, 'Ye shall receive power when the Holy Spirit is come upon you, and ye shall be my witnesses to the ends of the earth.' The fire baptism is definitely an endowment for service.

It is in souls who long to be as entirely separated to God's work as Christ was, who are ready to give themselves up to the Holy Spirit, as the Spirit of God's redeeming and saving grace, even as Christ did, that the fire baptism can effect God's purpose.

The two elements, the transformation of character, and the endowment for service, must not be separated; they are at best one. Many do separate them, and suffer loss. Some seek the transformed character, holiness of heart and life, while they make the service of God towards their fellowmen. But a very secondary thing. Others seek most earnestly the power, while a perfectly Christlike character is not earnestly aimed at. Both must fail. In Christ character and work were inseparable; His work had its worth from his life. In the power of the Spirit he obeyed and fulfilled God's will to the utmost – that gave his redeeming work its everlasting redeeming value. The eternal Spirit, through whom he offered himself to God for us, was the Spirit by whom he had allowed himself to be led every step of the way down even to the simple matter of his refusing to satisfy his hunger in the wilderness with bread which he provided himself. Character and service must grow out of one act. The root of all sin in us is one – selfishness. Whether it manifest itself in pleasing the flesh, or trusting in our own religion, or in coldness towards our fellowmen and neglect of the service God asks for them, it is the one thing we need to be delivered from. This is the hidden dross nothing but the fire baptism can reach and destroy. When the fire of God's holiness and God's love, when the fire that burnt in Christ and consumed him, baptises us – our devotion to God in holiness and to our fellowmen in service will be one.

What a difference between the Baptism of Water and of Fire! Alas, has not much of the ministry of the church, and the life of its believers, been far more a continuation of John's Water Baptism than of Christ's Fire Baptism! And had it but even been a faithful continuation of John's baptism – ever leading up to that which was with him first and last: He shall baptise with the Holy Ghost and with Fire!

Do we not, as we go along, at each step begin to feel: Ah, this is what we need, the Fire of God to fill our hearts as it fills heaven! If I am to live the holy life all the day long, and taste the blessedness of the clean in heart, nothing less than the Fire of God burning within continually is what I need. If I am to live tenderly, and work hopefully, amid all unworthiness and ingratitude, nothing less will do: I need the Fire of God. The Fire of God cleansing and keeping clean and holy, giving and maintaining Christ's own image and likeness! The Fire of God leading us, like him who baptises us with it, to follow on to Calvary in the one burning desire that God's honour may be restored in this his fallen world, and men may come again to bear the image and to know the unspeakable blessedness of the love of their God. We need the Baptism of Fire!

Chapter 5

The Two Baptisms: The Connection

'Wait for the promise of the Father, which, ye heard from me: For John indeed baptised with water: but ye shall be baptised with the Holy Ghost not many days hence.' Acts 1:4–5

The connection between these two baptisms – is it arbitrary and accidental, or are they parts of a living growth, an organic whole? God is a living God, and all his work in providence and redemption is pervaded by a living Spirit. The root bears the stem, the stem the branch, the branch the bud, and the bud the fruit, so each new advance in the kingdom of God has its roots in what preceded. The Water Baptism and the Fire Baptism are related as promise and fulfilment, as image and substance, a hope and the thing hoped for. All God's dealings with men are marked by these two stages. One finds it everywhere in the types and the history of the Old Testament. The whole connection of the Old Testament with the New shows how the principle underlines all God's revelation of himself to man. The history of the disciples before and after Pentecost illustrates its application to individual men. The experience in our day of many who can witness to a Second Blessing is proof that there may still be a conscious transition in the Christian life from an elementary stage to one of maturity or relative perfection.

The connection between the two baptisms is at root the same as between the two Testaments. In his redemption of the human race God accommodates himself to the law under which he placed the creature – the law of time and development, of slow growth and preparation, as the only way to a more advanced stage of maturity. When Adam fell, or Noah was saved, when Abraham was called, or Israel was brought out of Egypt, God might have sent his Son and wrought his great redemption. But it could not be. That fullness of time, of which God alone could judge, had to be accomplished. Every step in the slow path of preparation was a necessity. And so the Water Baptism, too, came to discover the utter insufficiency of all that is of earth and man, even though it has divine authority and sanction, and to waken the expectation of something supernatural and divine.

Of the certainty that every promise and every awakened expectation will have a divine fulfilment the Fire Baptism is thus the pledge. In the New Testament the prophecies of the Old have had a fulfilment passing all that the heart could conceive. The Son of God entering into our nature, his complete and everlasting victory over sin and Satan, his opening up of the heavenly world for us to enter in and dwell there, above all, his taking possession of the hearts of men and making them his and the Father's abode, that through them and out of them he might confirm the redeeming work on earth – all this was as high above all the thoughts of the Old Testament saints as the heavens are high above the earth. And even to those who are under the water baptism, with all the expectance that the Word and ordinances can awaken under the preparatory workings of the Spirit, can form no conception of what the experience of the Baptism of the Spirit and of Fire can be and do. The God who ordained the one as an earthly shadow and promise calls us to look to heaven and to himself for a direct revelation of his presence and power passing all understanding.

Still more remarkably the connection between the two baptisms is illustrated in the history of Christ's disciples. Have you ever thought what it means that just these men were chosen and counted fit to receive the great gift from heaven, and to dispense it to their fellowmen? Was there ever a general who undertook a great war with men who during a three years' campaign had failed in almost everything that could have won his confidence? Was there ever king ascended a throne and undertook to establish a kingdom with men as his counsellors and friends so utterly feeble and unreliable? And yet, it is just this that gives him his rule their glory, and gives us cause for confident and exultant hope. The great teaching of the Water Baptism was failure, confession, repentance, forgiveness: beyond that it could not go, for all else it pointed to the future. But in the future it did promise, in that word of infinite meaning, 'He shall baptise you with the Holy Spirit and with fire,' something that was to bring heaven unto men, and fill them with all the fullness of God. The work of the water baptism was simply to bring man to utter despair in himself, to large and living hope in God.

It is on this account that we need to look long and intensely on these men who first received the Holy Spirit from heaven. We are wont to look at all the incidents in their history separately, and to think that we know who and what they were. We need to gather up the many traits of their character into one, to trace all they were and did to its real source, and so to see, as in God's great object lesson, what really is the essential character of the Water Baptism in its relation to the glory that excelleth.

We shall find that all is comprised in the one word 'desire'. Desire is the moving spring of all life, the great motive power in the world. Desire leads men to work for their bread, or for riches, or for honour. It implies on the one hand a lack, on the other a hope. It is the heart feeling a need, fixing itself on the object that will satisfy that need. It was when the disciples had been brought to hate their own life, in which they had so shamefully grieved and forsaken their Lord, had been brought to love that life, as they had at the cross lost all their hope of him whom they had looked to as their Redeemer, that the life of God could in the Baptism of the Spirit take full possession of them. Desire, turning from the past and the present, turning from all in self and all even that God has provisionally wrought, to that full experience of his redeeming power which he has promised, intense, all-absorbing desire, waiting for the redemption in Israel, waiting for the promise of the Father, is the one great link between the Water Baptism and Fire Baptism. The one aim of the former is to prepare a soil in which the latter could do its blessed work.

Let all who are in personal search of the fullness of God's blessing note this well. Would you in your own experience understand the connection between the two stages in your spiritual life, the one of failure in which you live, the better one of power of which God speaks to you, hold fast the thought: the desire of the heart, that with all its strength turns itself from all that it has to receive all God has for it cannot be disappointed. There are some who have a desire for the fullness of the Spirit, but not as the only one thing they seek: it is only one desire among others. They have not turned away from everything of self, and the world, and the church. They must be disappointed. There are some who appear to despair of themselves and all around them, and seek to believe and claim the promise, and yet fail. It is nothing but the desire, which rules our whole being, that has not yet reached its full measure, and has not yet mastered the whole being. Why was it that in those who came to

Jesus on earth for healing for themselves or others, their faith never failed to accept his word? The reason was simply this: the intensity of their desire prepared them with their whole heart to believe. The leper, and the blind, and the lame, knew what it was they desired above everything. Christ's word found an open heart. Let us beware of thinking that we desire it intensely enough. Let us yield ourselves to the teaching and action of the preparatory work of God's Spirit in conviction, and waiting: the desire wholly set, in despair of self and trust in God, on the fullness of the Spirit, must be fulfilled.

This connection between the two baptisms is nothing but what is seen in the way by which those are led who can witness to the reality of second blessing. There has come to them an intense dissatisfaction with all that in their religious life and work they have yet obtained. Others may count them far advanced, there may be much which they know is God's own work in them, and which they praise him yet for, but they have found in the word the promise and the prospect of a rest and a joy and a presence, of a strength and a nearness of God which they do not know. And nothing can satisfy them till they do. They know that God's Spirit is in them, and most fervently do they seek to be faithful to his leadings and gracious enablings. But just as all God's interventions and deliverances of old on behalf of his people proceeded to a fullness of time when he should come in whom all the fullness dwells, and out of whose fullness we should receive, so they believed that in personal experience, too, there is a fullness of time when the Holy Spirit comes with a directness and an abiding consciousness, and an all-pervading power of which nothing but Pentecost can give a conception. And there have been those who have testified that one hour of that presence, 'above all sense and reason', as taught and wrought more than many years of earnest and prayerful service could give. It is with them even as with the disciples, all the blessed experiences of the Master's presence with them, of his gracious words, and his mighty works, were as nothing compared to that day when, as the glorified one, he came down and entered into them. No wonder they continued daily with one accord in the temple, praising God.

Let all who long for the full revelation of God in their heart hold fast the living connection between the two stages. The water baptism of John is from God in heaven, a spiritual nursery and training school for his young children. Its one central thought is: it points to, it prepares for, it promises the Baptism of the Spirit of Fire. It is not without the Spirit: how could it be of God, or do God's work, or prepare for the full indwelling of the Spirit, if it were not of the Spirit, and its children not under his charge. Just as the New Testament is enfolded in the Old, and the Old enfolded in the New, because they testify of one Christ, so the Fire Baptism lies enfolded in the Water Baptism, because they are the two-fold presence of one Spirit. The Water Baptism, the messenger pointing to the one great promise of the Father, is the one great preparation for its reception.

Let the attitude of all who would know fully that the blessing is simply that of intense desire of the fulfilment of the promise rooted in faith in him who gave it. Look up above and see the Father ever pouring out into the Son the fullness of his Spirit for his people. Look up and see the Son ever pouring upon and out into his people the fullness of the Spirit on the receiver. Look up until everything vanishes out of sight in view of the promise of the Father. Look up and see the longing of the loving heart of Jesus as he desires after most perfect and inti-mate and abiding union with you. Look up until your whole heart be desire. The sense of not having what you can have and must have, the acknowledgement that nothing in you or the Church around you can give it, the assurance that he who baptised with the Holy Spirit has it to give and will give it.

The Africa Evangelical Fellowship

The AEF is an international evangelical mission. For more information about their work, please contact them at their International office, 17 Westcote Road, Reading, Berks RG3 2DL.

The AEF has hundreds of opportunities for both long and short term service in evangelism, church planting, education, medical administration, youth work and other practical fields.

Other AEF offices are:-

Australia
PO Box 292
Castle Hill
New South Wales 2154

Zimbabwe
99 Gaydon Road
Graystone Park
Borrowdale
Harare

Canada
470 McNicoll Avenue
Willowdale
Ontario M2H 2E1

South Africa
Rowland House
6 Montrose Avenue
Claremont 7700

USA
PO Box 2896
Boone
North Carolina 28607

New Zealand
PO Box 1390
Invercargill

United Kingdom
30 Lingfield Road
Wimbledon
London SW19 4PU

Europe
5 Rue de Meautry
94500 Champigny-sur-Marne
France